Treasury of PROVERBS & EPIGRAMS

AVENEL BOOKS

NEW YORK

This edition is published by Avenel Books,
distributed by Crown Publishers, Inc., by arrangement with
Ottenheimer Publishers, Inc.

Previously published as *Proverbs and Epigrams*

Manufactured in the United States of America

Library of Congress Cataloging in Publication Data

ISBN: 0-517-117754 (library edition)
0-517-381346 (suede edition)

o   n   m   l   k   j

List of Authorities Quoted

(Indicated in the Text by Corresponding Numbers.)

Subject Guide

Preface

Proverbs and epigrams form the nucleus of the wisdom of man. Those contained in this book have been handed down through the ages by the great philosophers and teachers in the history of our world!

While some of these men and women have all but been forgotten, their words are as fresh and new today as when first spoken; and their wisdom has grown and ripened with the passing of time.

You who read this book can not help but reap rich rewards in knowledge and wisdom that will aid you as you go through life.

The World's Best Proverbs and Epigrams

This World.

This world that we're a livin' in
　　Is mighty hard to beat;
You get a thorn with every rose,
　　But ain't the roses sweet?

On Wishing as a Pastime.

Wishing of all employments is the worst!
Philosophy's reverse and health's decay!　(8)
In idle wishes fools supinely stay:
Be there a will—and wisdom finds a way.　(170)

Wishing is an expedient to be poor.　(8)

Wishers and Woulders are never good householders.

Wishes never filled the bag.

I never fared worse than when I wished for my supper.

A man must keep his mouth open a long while before a roast pigeon flies into it.

With wishing comes grieving.

Many of our wishes have been and will be thwarted.　(6)

Our very wishes (when realized) give us not our wish.　(8)

Early successes are mostly rather according to wish than wisdom.　(6)

What ardently we wish we soon believe.　(8)

No wise man ever wishes to be younger.　(17)

Our blunders mostly come from letting our wishes interpret our duties.　(123)

Wish chastely and love dearly.　(75)

Alas! what a number of desires have come to nothing!

1

On the Advantages Secured by the Diligently Slothful, the Persistently Idle and the Incurably Lazy.

When inertia gets the better of you it is time to telephone to the undertaker.   (257)

The only real neutral in this game of life is a dead one.
(257)

He is idle that might be better employed.
Idleness is the sepulchre of a living man.   (151)

Idleness is the devil's bolster.
Idle folks have the least leisure.
Standing pools gather filth.
Of idleness comes no goodness.
By doing nothing we learn to do ill.
To do nothing teaches to do evil.
Doing nothing is doing ill.
The man with time to burn never gave the world any light.
He becometh poor that dealeth with a slack hand.   (27)

Idle folks lack no excuses.
Idleness is the root of all evil.
Idleness rusts the mind.
Idleness must thank itself if it goes barefoot.
Enjoyment stops where indolence begins.   (9)

Sloth is the mother of poverty.
Idleness teacheth much evil.   (10)

Idle folks have the most labor.
Idleness always envies industry.
Idleness is the greatest prodigality in the world.
That work which is begun well is half done.   (111)

He that is slothful in his work is brother to him that is a great waster.   (27)

You'll soon learn to shape Idle a coat.
All days are short to Industry and long to Idleness.
Success sits throned beyond two "Swinging Doors," ("Pull" one, "Push" two).

Her Waiting Rooms are always crowded full (By such as You).

Scores get there by the Door marked "Push," and some
Gain entrance by the other Door marked "Pull."

Love not sleep, lest thou come to poverty. (27)

A young man idle, an old man needy. (70)

They must hunger in frost that will not work in heat.

Slothfulness casteth into a deep sleep, and an idle soul shall suffer hunger. (27)

A girl unemployed is thinking of mischief.

Absence of occupation is not rest. (7)

A mind quite vacant is a mind distress'd. (7)

If the devil catch a man idle he'll set him to work.

The slothful man saith, There is a lion without, I shall be slain in the streets. (27)

The lazy servant, to save one step, goes eight.

There is more trouble in having nothing to do than in having much to do.

People who have nothing to do are quickly tired of their own company. (66)

They must hunger in frost who springtime have lost.

An idler is a watch that wants both hands;
As useless if it goes as when it stands. (7)

He that sleepeth in harvest is a son that causeth shame. (27)

When we do ill the devil tempteth us; when we do nothing we tempt him.

As lazy as Ludlam's dog that leaned his head against the wall to bark.

To be idle and unemployed is a sign not only of a weak head, but of a bad heart. (107)

The desire of the slothful killeth him, for his hands refuse to labor. (27)

He that is idle, and followeth after vain persons, shall have enough; but how? "Shall have enough of poverty." (1)

A sluggard takes an hundred steps because he would not take one in due time.

Yet a little sleep, a little slumber, a little folding of the hands to sleep; so shall thy poverty come as a robber, and thy want as an armed man. (207)

You saddle today and ride out tomorrow.

Nor suffer idle sloth to lean upon thy charitable arm. (62)

3

An idle person is the devil's playfellow.
A slothful man is a beggar's brother.
A slothful man never has time.
At evening the sluggard is busy.
What better is the house for a sluggard's early rising?
He slumbers enough who does nothing.
Nothing falls into the mouth of a sleeping fox.
An idle brain is the devil's workshop.

> A good for nothing lazy lout,
> Wicked within and ragged without.
> Who can bear to have him about?
> Turn him out! Turn him out!

A lazy spirit is a losing spirit.
A pound of idleness weighs twenty ounces.
A slothful hand makes a slender estate.
What heart can think or tongue express
The harm that comes of idleness?
Laziness travels so slowly that poverty soon overtakes him.
Laziness is nothing unless you carry it out.
Laziness begins with cobwebs and ends with iron chains.
It is a great weariness to do nothing.
Idle people are dead people that you can't bury.
Idle bodies are generally busybodies.
Don't live in Idleburgh.
He who is doing nothing is seldom without helpers.
There is always room at the top if you can push the other fellow off.

On Some of the Disadvantages Experienced by the Few Who are Energetic and Lovers of Hard Work.

The man of power is one who wrings success out of the stony heart of defeat. In fact he does not show his true colors until he has rid himself of the friendship of the many. The man of power is what he is, and his personality makes itself felt wherever he goes. (257)

'Tis deeds must win the prize. (32)

The mill gains by going, and not by standing still.
The living rock is worn by the diligent flow of the brook.
(62)

4

Deeds are fruits, words are but leaves.

You never know what you can do till you try. (123)

Put a stout heart to a steep hill.

Few things seem so possible as they are till they are attempted. (6)

There is a wonderful power in honest work to develop latent energies and reveal a man to himself. (123)

Industry is the parent of success.

Good fortune is the offspring of our endeavors, although there be nothing sweeter than ease.

Defeated men are the only ones who succeed—read history —because defeat means the disapproval of the mediocre, and the enmity of the chuckleheaded. No really great man has ever been able to carry his own district twice in succession, and usually not even once. (257)

No life can be dreary when work is delight. (64)

It is glad labor which is ordinarily productive of labor.

(123)

Care and diligence bring luck.

As is the workman so is the work.

If pains be a pleasure to you profit will follow.

Labor overcometh all things.

There are no gains without pains; then help hands, for I have no lands.

Goods acquired by industry prove commonly more lasting than lands by descent. (1)

God gives all things to industry.

Business is a fight—a continual struggle—just as life is. Man has reached his present degree of development through struggle. Struggle there must be and always will be.

The man who consecrates his hours
By vig'rous effort and an honest aim,
At once he draws the sting of life and death;
He walks with Nature, and her paths are peace. (8)

Our wisdom and our duty is to work and not to faint. (62)

In all labor there is profit; but the tall of the lips tendeth only to penury. (27)

Industry is the parent of virtue.

So there be not mischief in thy toil, thou gainest, as a conqueror of sloth.

Employment brings enjoyment.

It is a very waste of life to be and not to do. (62)

Think of ease but work on.

Not what I have but what I do is my kingdom. (33)

The end of all is an action, not a thought, though it were of the noblest. (33)

No man is born into the World whose Work is not born with him. There is always Work, and lots of it withal, for those who will—and blessed are the Horny Hands of toil. (139)

Crown every passing day with some good action daily. (62)

He that gathereth by labor shall increase. (27)

What to thought a veil must prove
That an action may remove,
Thus by doing you shall know
What it is you have to do. (6)

Labor—all labor is noble and holy. (29)

The hand of the diligent maketh rich. (27)

Usefulness comes by labor, wit by ease. (4)

Labor hath sweet uses, labor sanctifieth all things;
Adding brightness, flavor, beauty, even to the humblest.
(62)

Labor has a bitter root, but a sweet taste.

He that gathereth in summer is a wise son. (27)

It has been said the meek shall inherit the earth, but we all want the earth nowadays and I know that it is not the meek who get the earth these days. (265)

While ten men watch *chances* one man *makes chances.* While ten men wait for something to *turn up* one man *turns something up.* So, while ten men *fail* one succeeds, and is called a man of *luck*, the favorite of fortune. There is no luck like *pluck*, and fortune favors those most who are most indifferent to fortune.

When industry goes out of the door poverty comes in at the window.

How many, better in their graves, work hard for wrong and harm, with misdirected energies and ill-applied exertion. (62)

There are no gains without pains; then plough deep while sluggards sleep.

We develop the resources of the world, and mature and discipline our own powers by endeavor. (6)

Attempt the end, and never stand to doubt;
Nothing's so hard but search will find it out. (22)

Work as if thou hadst to live for aye;
Worship as if thou wert to die today. (132)

Give not sleep to thine eyes, nor slumber to thine eyelids. Deliver thyself as a roe from the hand of the hunter, and as a bird from the hand of the fowler. (27)

Put your own shoulder to the wheel.

On Income and Expenditure, Borrowing, Debt, Wealth and Poverty.

There is no surer test of integrity than a well-proportioned expenditure. (38)

Live within your means.

Better go to bed supperless than rise in debt.

Only that which is honestly got is gain.

Moderate your expenses now, at first, as you may keep the same proportion still; nor stand so much on your gentility. (114)

Riches have wrought me here sadness of mind:
When I rely on them, lo! they depart,—
Bitterly—fie on them!—rend they my heart. (162)

Living upon trust is the way to pay double.

A man in debt is caught in a net.

An honest darn is better than debt.

First comes owing, and then comes lying.

It is hard to pay for bread that has been eaten.

Debt is the worst poverty.

Debt is an evil conscience.

Be not made a beggar by banqueting upon borrowing. (10)

He is rich enough who owes nothing.

The greatest wealth is contentment with a little.

If you pay what you owe, what you're worth you'll know.

Ready money works great cures.

A good wife and health are a man's best wealth.

He who is ashamed of his poverty would be equally proud of his wealth.

Money is a good servant, but a dangerous master. (122)

Little and often fills the purse.

Riches avail not in the day of wrath. (1)

Riches are like muck, which stink in a heap, but spread abroad, make the earth fruitful.

That corrupteth which we hoard. (63)

When you have bought one fine thing, you must buy ten more that your appearance may be all of a piece.

Spending your money with many a guest empties the kitchen, the cellar, and chest.

Pay quickly that thou owest. The needy tradesman is made glad by such considerate haste;

Pay duly also those other petty gifts, the letter, or the visit, or the gift. (62)

He is rich that is satisfied.

Many have been ruined by buying good bargains.

Ready money is ready medicine.

At a great bargain make a pause.

A light purse makes a heavy heart.

A penny saved is a penny earned.

According to your purse govern your mouth.

An empty purse frights away friends.

Ask thy purse when thou shouldst buy.

He that buys what he does not want must often sell what he does want.

Who heeds not a penny shall never have any.

He is richest that has fewest wants.

Give and spend and God will send.

A full purse makes the mouth run over.

A good bargain is a pick-purse

A bad thing is dear at any price.

Always taking out of the meal-tub and never putting in, soon comes to the bottom.

Well-got wealth may meet disaster, but ill-got wealth destroys its master.

Much would have more and lost all.

Where the treasure is there the heart is.

From a bad paymaster get what you can.

Cheap is dear in the long run.

Not to oversee workmen is to leave them your purse open.

Grasp all—lose all.

Don't reckon your chickens before they are hatched.

Gain gotten by a lie will burn one's fingers.

He that has but four and spends five has no need of a purse.

Cut your coat according to your cloth.

Everyone is kin to the rich man.

He who loses money loses much; he who loses a friend loses more; but he who loses courage loses all.

Ill fares the land, to hastening ills a prey,
Where wealth accumulates—and men decay;
Princes and lords may flourish or may fade—
A breath can make them, as a breath has made;
But a bold peasantry, their country's pride,
When once destroyed, can never be supplied.   (3)

On Economy and Waste.

Waste makes want.

Frugality is an estate.

Economy is a great revenue.

Of all prodigality, that of time is the worst.

Waste not, want not.

You know the old proverb—pay as you go—unless you are going for good.

A good driver turns in a small space.

A good saver is a good server.

Rust wastes more than use.

A fat kitchen makes a lean will.

A favor ill-placed is great waste.

Some savers in a house do well.

He who begins and does not finish loses his labor.

After one that earns comes one that wastes.

He who saves in little things can be liberal in great ones.

The most important element in success is economy—economy of money and time.

He that does not save pennies will never have dollars.

If your means suit not with your ends, pursue those ends which suit with your means.

Take care to be an economist in prosperity; there is no fear of your being one in adversity. (116)

See a pin and let it lie, you'll want a pin before you die.

Make no expense, but to do good to others or yourself; that is, waste nothing. (14)

The great question is, not so much what money you have in your pocket, as what you will buy with it. (44)

For want of a nail the shoe is lost; for want of a shoe the horse is lost; and for want of a horse the man is lost.

Thrift is better than an annuity.

He shall never want more who is thankful for, and thrifty with a little. (1)

The true philosopher's stone is to have means and not to spend injudiciously.

The harvest and vintage come not every day, therefore be provident.

Not possession but use is the only riches.

From saving comes having.

A man's purse will never be bare,
If he knows when to buy, to spend, and to spare.

On Some Contrasts and Comparisons.

Better leave than lack.

Who shuts his hand hath lost his gold,
Who opens it hath it twice told. (4)

A man of pleasure is a man of pains. (8)

Most haste, worst speed!

Great boaster, little doer.

Labor warms, sloth harms.

Hot love is soon cold.

A thorn is a changed bud. (6)

The handsomest flower is not the sweetest.

As is the gardener so is the garden.

What is enough was never little.

He who decries wants to buy.

Who knows most says least.
Who loves well chastises well.
To err is human, to forgive divine.   (2)
Obedience is better than sacrifice.
Persuasion is better than force.
Nature requires little—fancy much.
Beauty and folly are often companions.
Much religion, but no goodness.
The beaten path is the safest.
Much praying, but no piety.
He is the greatest conqueror who has conquered himself.
Small faults indulged let in greater.
Better an egg today than a hen tomorrow.
Better a blush on the face than a spot in the heart.
Truth individualizes, love unites.   (6)

The lion had need of the mouse.
Angels their failings—mortals have their praise.   (8)

One is na sae soon heal'd as hurt.   (69)

A face of pleasure but a heart of pain.   (5)

The worst wheel always creaks most.
A man of straw needs a woman of gold.
Better the child cry than the old man.
Better the child cry than the mother sigh.
Be swift to hear, and with patience give answer.   (10)

The heart of a fool is in his mouth, but the mouth of a
wise man is in his heart.   (133)

He buys honey dear who has to lick it off thorns.
A little neglect may breed great mischief.
What the fool does in the end the wise man does in the
beginning.   (99)

A man that hideth his foolishnes is better than a man that
hideth his wisdom.   (10)

It is easier to stem the brook than the river.
There are errors near akin to truth, and wholesomes linked
with poisons.   (62)

It is beautiful to see an injured, disappointed man, protec-
tive and kindly.   (6)

The dearer the child the sharper must be the rod.

Of listening children have your fears, for little pitchers have great ears.

In the land of the blind the one-eyed is a king.

In prosperity caution—in adversity patience.

One often has need of a lesser than oneself.

There are more foolish buyers than foolish sellers.

No greater promisers than they who have nothing to give.

The good seaman is known in bad weather.

There is as much greatness in owning a good turn as in doing it.

Better once in heaven than ten times at the gate.

The moth does most mischief to the finest garment.

Best wine cometh at the last;—the King to end the pageant.
(62)

A fair skin often covers a crooked mind.

More people are slain by suppers than by the sword.

Father and mother are kind, but God is kinder.

Resolve slowly, act swiftly; a quiet eye for the quick hand.
(62)

Better to deny at once than to promise long.

Better lose your labor than your time in idleness.

No office so humble, but it is better than nothing.

Be suspicious of the good which wicked men can praise.
(62)

Better alone than in bad company.

A handsome shoe often pinches the foot.

Good words without deeds are rushes and reeds.

Handsome women generally fall to the lot of ugly men.

Who has love in his heart has spurs in his sides.

Mighty hearts are held in slender chains. (2)

The joys of sense to mental joys are mean. (8)

Folly's shallow lips can ask the deepest question. (62)

A little body doth often harbor a great soul.

Who paints me before blackens me behind.

The pains of mind surpass the pains of sense. (8)

Little dogs start the hare, but great ones catch it.

Little sticks kindle the fire, but great ones put it out.

Be not hasty in thy tongue, and in thy deeds slack and remiss. (10)

To a hasty demand a leisure reply.

Though the speaker be a fool, let the hearer be wise.

When I did well, I heard it never; when I did ill, I heard it ever.

Cloudy mornings turn to clear evenings.

He that speaks doth sow, he that holds his peace doth reap.

They who love most are least valued.

Wise men learn by other men's mistakes, fools by their own.

The generous man enriches himself by giving; the miser hoards himself poor.

A wholesome tongue is a tree of life; but perverseness therein is a breach in the spirit.   (27)

Better is the mass of men, suspicion, than thy fears.

Kinder than thy thoughts, O chilling heart of prudence.

Purer than thy judgments, ascetic tongue of censure.

In all things worthier to love, if not also wiser to esteem.

(62)

A soft answer turneth away wrath, but grievous words stir up anger.   (27)

He that is slow to wrath is of great understanding, but he that is hasty of spirit exalteth folly.   (27)

The true creed solely in the head and the false creed noways in the heart.

Maketh good neutral in the first, maketh evil neutral in the second.   (62)

Most true a wise man never will be sad;

But neither will sonorous, bubbling mirth,

A shallow stream of happiness betray.   (8)

I have seen many rich burdened with the fear of poverty;

I have seen many poor, buoyed with all the carelessness of wealth;

For the rich had the spirit of a pauper, and the moneyless a liberal heart;

The first enjoyeth not for having, and the latter hath nothing but enjoyment.

None is poor but the mean in mind, the timorous, the weak and unbelieving;

None is wealthy but the affluent in soul, who is satisfied and floweth over.

The poor-rich is attenuate for fears; the rich-poor is fattened upon hopes;

Cheerfulness is one man's welcome, and the other warneth from him by his gloom. (62)

Every wise woman buildeth her house, but the foolish plucketh it down with her hands. (27)

For a rich man to be frugal is to prove unfaithful to his trust,

While for the poor man to be prodigal is presumptuous, as sinning against prudence. (62)

He that falls into sin is a man; that grieves at it, is a saint; that boasteth of it is a devil. (1)

When it comes to a show-down in America the Golden Rule stands small chance in competition with the Big Stick. (257)

For what is vice? Self-love in a mistake;
A poor blind merchant buying joys too dear;
And virtue what? 'Tis self-love in her wits—
Quite skillful in the market of delight. (8)

One goeth homeward from his toil to rest and peace and plenty,

Greeted on the threshold by his cleanly goodwife's kiss;

His neighbor meanwhile met by that old slattern left at home

With the quick hailstorm of her tongue in quarreling and worry. (62)

Judge how wide the limits stand
Between a splendid and a happy land. (3)

Knowledge humbleth the great man, astonisheth the common man, and puffeth up the little man.

There is an economy that sinneth, never dropping largesse kindly,

As there is an erring prodigality pandering to luxury and sloth. (62)

The wicked sin, the godly smart, most in this world. (1)

Much learning shows how little mortals know;
Much wealth, how little worldlings can enjoy. (8)

14

Men often are of a sad heart, yet of a hopeful word and endeavor. (6)

Love with life is heaven; and life unloving, hell. (62)

The Most High God sees, and bears; my neighbor knows nothing, and yet is always finding fault. (75)

Faith opens a way for the understanding, unbelief closes it. (39)

There is much novelty that is without hope, much antiquity without sacredness. (6)

One eye of the master sees more than four of the servant's.
(70)

If the doctor cures, the sun sees it; but if he kills the earth hides it. (69)

The epicure puts his purse into his belly; and the miser his belly into his purse.

Friends are ever dearer in thy wealth, but relations to be trusted in thy need,

For these are God's appointed way, and those the choice of man.

There is a lower warmth in kin, but smaller truth in friends. The latter show more surface, and the first have more of depth.

Relations rally to the rescue, even in estrangement and neglect, where friends will have fled at thy defeat, even after promise and kindness. (62)

There is a shame that bringeth sin; and there is a shame which is glory and grace. (10)

Mercy, in her love refuses;
Most merciful, as oft, when seeming least!
Most gracious when she seemed the most to frown. (9)

Men can write perfect ethical systems, but nevertheless they cannot stand being watched when they go out at night. (265)

The heart of fools is in their mouth, but the mouth of the wise is in their heart. (10)

A knotty piece of timber must have smooth wedges.
Failure is success to thee if thou could'st read all truth.
(62)

It is easier to run fast for a minute than to grind along the dusty road for a day. (123)

15

Let not thine hand be stretched out to receive and shut when thou shouldst repay. (10)

You pay more for your schooling than your learning is worth.

As the smell of the sea cleaves to the sea-plant for long years so the love of the dead clings to the living. (6)

To give is easier than to love, to be praised more sweet than praising.

Your great philanthropist is found, scattering money charities; far off, far off, to the antipodes—but seldom to the heathen at   door.

And folks live out long life-times, near dwellers in one hamlet unheedful of each other, though they worship in one church. (62)

The treasures which are kept in coffers are not real, but only those which are kept in the soul. (123)

Reason's progressive, instinct is complete;
Swift instinct leaps, slow reason feebly climbs. (8)

Who lives to nature rarely can be poor—who lives to fancy never can be rich. (8)

Infancy is wakeful as the lark, though its early song is not always so pleasing as the bird's. (6)

Where the world rebuketh there look out for the excellent. (62)

The fairest life ever lived on earth was that of a poor man and with all its beauty it moved within the limits of narrow resources. (123)

In love losing ourselves we find ourselves; and it is proved to us that self-blessedness is best realized by self-abandonment. (6)

In Time we only can begin—Eternity must deal with ends. (62)

There is that scattereth, and yet increaseth; and there is that withholdeth more than is meet, but it tendeth to poverty. (27)

Let the misanthrope shun men and abjure, the most are rather lovable than hateful. (62)

False pleasure from abroad her joys imports;
Rich from within, and self-sustained the true;

The true is fixed and solid as a rock;
Slippery the false, and tossing as the wave. (8)

On Husbands and Wives—Courtship and Marriage and What is Often Preferred, or Should be—Celibacy.

Probably you are going to say that two people can live on less than one. If they do, it is because they have to.
Wedlock is a padlock.
Single life is often guilty of freedom. (62)
Always say no, and you will never be married.
She that weds well will wisely match her love,
Nor be below her husband—nor above. (169)
A cheerful wife is the joy of life.
Choose your love, and then love your choice.
Don't be in a hurry to tie what you can't untie.
If your wife is crust, mind that you are crumb.
Before you run in double harness look well to the other horse.
Let every husband stay a lover true,
And every wife remain a sweetheart too.
A good husband makes a good wife.
A bad husband cannot be a good man.
It is not every couple that is a pair.
A bad wife likes her husband's heel to be towards home.
Before your youth with marriage is oppressed,
Make choice of one who suits your humor best;
Such choicest damsel drops not from the sky,
She must be sought for with a studious eye. (169)
He that takes a wife takes care. (14)
A world of comfort lies in that one word, wife. (136)
He who marries for wealth sells his own liberty.
A good wife and health are a man's best wealth.
A good wife is a good prize.
Choose a wife rather by your ear than your eye.
Be sure before you marry of a house wherein to tarry.
Before you marry consider what you do.
Ne'er seek a wife till ye ken what to do wi' her.
The wedding should last through wedded life.

Discreet wives have sometimes neither eyes nor ears.

An obedient wife commands her husband.

In marriage it is all very well to say that "the two are made one"—the question is *which one?*

A bonny bride is soon buskit (dressed). (69)

He who has a good wife can bear any evil.

He who does not honor his wife dishonors himself. (99)

Who has a bad wife, his hell begins on earth.

You may beat the de'il into your wife, but you'll never bang him out again.

What shall compensate a wife for a home despoiled of love?

> Home love is a woman's very life; a man may live without it.

> The mother-bird hath one poor nest; foxes have holes elsewhere.

A man's best fortune, or his worst, is a wife.

Mated opposites contend; unmated concords pine. (62)

He who has a bad wife can expect no happiness that can be so called.

The woman's occupation and her mission is to have a home other than her father's and knit with dearer ties. (62)

Who weds a sot to get his cot will lose his cot and keep the sot.

What martyrdom for gentle wives—once married to bad husbands! (62)

Blessed is the man that hath a virtuous wife, for the number of his days shall be double. (10)

Take heed that what charmeth thee is real, nor springeth of thine own imagination; and suffer not trifles to win thy love. (62)

It is a sorry house in which the cock is silent and the hen crows.

When the husband earns well the wife spins well.

Who can guess the potency of woman's love and patience, her precious influence, her sweet strength, to bless a husband's home? (62)

Wisdom in the man, patience in the wife, bring peace to the house, and a happy life.

He drives a good wagonful into his farm who gets a good wife.

Silver weddings may have been, but more are forged of iron, though few dare hint hard truths like these, and flatter or ignore them. (62)

Neither reproach nor flatter thy wife where anyone heareth or seeth it.

So many miserable mistakes, and all without a cure!—The wrong sort idly won, the right sort left unwooed. (62)

Smoke, floods, and a troublesome wife are enough to drive a man out of his life.

In Paradise, before the fall, God instituted marriage, and Jesus first wrought miracles to bless a wedding feast. (62)

When the husband is fire, and the wife tow, the devil easily sets them in a flame.

A woman that will not comfort her husband in distress maketh weak hands and feeble knees. (10)

The man is made by gentleness, that meek and quiet spirit; The holy conversation and obedience of the wife; The man is marred by crossings and the nagging vixen temper; Night and day, by board and bed, embittered through that plague; No escape, no respite, for the worm is at the core; An exile cannot flee himself, nor hounds in leash run freely; Who shall gauge the force of such a spiritual fetter, Hindering all pursuit of good, and galling and injurious? (62)

For the multitude whose hope is selfish, worldly happiness, such fare not better singly, than those that missed it doubly. (62)

Woe to the sensitive and gentle in their married lives! Provocation, irritation, usurpation, iteration, vacillation, accusation, every phase of malice in every note of harshness—Prejudices, jealousies and strifes, contention, hate, confusion. Every phase of ill from weakness up to wickedness,—All these have often cursed the home through ill-assorted marriage, and many wives and husbands here will own they read their fates. (62)

Don't put your finger into too tight a ring.
Some seek for discussion, and trouble, and strife;
Like a dog and a cat live such man and wife. (12)

The good or ill hap of a good or ill life, is the good or ill choice of a good or ill wife.

Who wives for a dower resigns his own power.

On Woman.

To a Grass Widow: Go chase yourself—I won't! (257)

And very rightly the question comes in; if marriage is a lottery, why don't they arrest the minister? (257)

> As unto the bow the cord is,
> So unto the man is woman,
> Though she bends him she obeys him,
> Though she draws him, yet she follows,
> Useless each without the other. (12)

A woman who looks much in the glass spins but little.

The handsomest woman can only give what she has.

The weeping bride makes a laughing wife.

A fine girl and a tattered gown always find something to hook them.

A woman that paints puts up a bill: "To let."

The foolish woman is clamorous; she is simple and knoweth nothing.

> One hair of a woman draws more than a bell-rope. (103)

She is noblest, being good. (147)

Whatever may be the customs and laws of a country, the women of it decide the morals. (150)

Woman may be a fickle thing, but it is where the captivation is of her fancy—not of her heart. (153)

Women are the poetry of the world. (148)

Every wise woman buildeth her house; but the foolish plucketh it down with her own hands. (27)

A virtuous woman is a crown to her husband; but she that doeth shamefully is as rottenness to the bones. (27)

A virtuous woman, though ugly, is the ornament of the house.

> She doeth little kindnesses,
> Which most leave undone, or despise. (139)

She is the good man's paradise, and the bad's
First step to heaven. (146)

The world was sad! the garden was a wild!
And man, the hermit, sigh'd—till woman smiled! (143)

Adam laid him down and slept—and from his side
    A woman in her magic beauty rose;
Dazzled and charm'd, he call'd that woman bride,
    And his first sleep became his last repose. (145)

    Life hath no dim and lowly spot
    That doth not in her sunshine share. (139)

Though men may fall in love with girls at play, there is
nothing to make them stand to their love like seeing them at
work. (135)

Adorn'd by the bay, or enwreathed with the willow,
Her smile is our meed and her bosom our pillow. (152)

A woman's idea of a square deal is one in which she comes
out ahead.

Some men prefer long office hours because it shortens their
hours at home.

While making hats for women the spinster milliner may be
setting her cap for a man.

Women's curiosity has been doing a continuous performance
ever since Mother Eve took a bite of that little apple.

Women have more strength in their looks than we have
in our laws, and more power in their tears than we have by our
arguments. (149)

The man after a woman's own heart may not want it.

    A virtuous woman is a splendid prize;
    A bad—the greatest curse beneath the skies.

A handsome woman is soon dressed.

O! they love least who let men know their love. (32)

A man is as good as he has to be, and a woman is as bad
as she dares. (257)

To be man's tender mate was woman born,
And in obeying Nature she best serves
The purposes of Heaven. (144)

        If ladies be but young and fair,
        They have the gift to know it. (32)

A "fine lady" is but a painted sepulchre for a man to bury his happiness in. (6)

The gaudy gossip, when she's set agog,
In jewels drest, and at each ear a bob,
Goes flaunting out, and in her train of pride
Thinks all she says or does is justified. (37)

How few are lovely that are made for love!
Do you, my fair, endeavour to possess
An elegance of mind as well as dress? (142)

Yet, lovely woman! yet, thy winning smile
That caused our cares can every care beguile. (95)

When female cheeks refuse to glow,
Farewell to virtue here below;
Maintain your modesty and station,
So women shall preserve the nation. (151)

She hath done what she could. Wheresoever this Gospel shall be preached throughout the whole world, this also that she hath done shall be spoken of for a memorial of her. (158)

Fair ladies! you drop manna in the way of starved people.
(32)

It is no pilgrimage to travel to your lips. (141)

Fair, good, rich, and wise, is a woman four stories high.

Kind words and few are a woman's ornament.

Nothing makes a woman more esteemed by the opposite sex than chastity. (120)

Every one that looketh on a woman to lust after her hath committed adultery with her already in his heart. (158)

God causes the good woman's purpose to prosper.

A woman that feareth the Lord she shall be praised.

The world waits for love—the vigilance of love, the service of love, the sacrifice of love. (263)

The girl whom benevolence warms
Is an angel who lives but to bless. (106)

Let no man value at a little price a virtuous woman's counsel. (134)

Nothing lovelier can be found in woman, than to study household good, and good works in her husband to promote.
(26)

She who does not make her family comfortable will herself never be happy at home, and she who is not happy at home will never be happy anywhere. (120)

Good housewife provides, ere a sickness do come,
Of sundry good things in her house to have some. (140)

'Tis virtue that doth make them most admired;
'Tis modesty that makes them seem divine. (32)

Women are never so amiable as when they are useful. (135)

The foundation of domestic happiness is faith in the virtue of woman. (76)

A cross-grained woman and a snappish dog take care of the house.

A virtuous woman! her price is far above rubies.

The heart of her husband doth safely trust in her, so that he shall have no need of spoil;

She will do him good and not evil all the days of her life;

She seeketh wool and flax, and worketh willingly with her hands;

She is like the merchant's ships; she bringeth her food from afar;

She riseth also while it is yet night, and giveth meat to her household, and a portion to her maidens.

She considereth a field and buyeth it: with the fruit of her hands she planteth a vineyard.

She girdeth her loins with strength, and strengtheneth her arms;

She perceiveth that her merchandise is good: her candle goeth not out by night;

She layeth her hands to the spindle, and her hands hold the distaff:

She stretcheth out her hand to the poor; yea, she reacheth forth her hands to the needy;

She is not afraid of the snow for her household: for all her household are clothed with scarlet;

She maketh herself coverings of tapestry; her clothing is silk and purple;

Her husband is known in the gates, when he sitteth among the elders of the land.

She maketh fine linen and selleth it; and delivereth girdles
unto the merchants;

Strength and honor are her clothing, and she shall rejoice
in time to come;

She openeth her mouth with wisdom; and in her tongue is
the law of kindness;

She looketh well to the ways of her household, and eateth
not the bread of idleness;

Her children arise up, and call her blessed; her husband
also, and he praiseth her: "Many daughters have done
virtuously, but thou excellest them all!"

Give her of the fruit of her hands, and let her own works
praise her in the gates. (27)

When the fulness of the time came God sent forth His Son,
born of a woman. (41)

The seed of the woman shall bruise the head of the serpent.

On Beauty and Deformity.

Woman's beauty, the forest echo, and rainbows soon pass
away.

Beauty is a blossom.

Beauty is no inheritance.

Beauty without merit and virtue is a bait for fools. (21)

Beauty is but skin deep.

Beauty buys no beef.

Mock not at those who are misshapen by nature. (1)

Beauty draws more than oxen.

A thing of beauty is a joy for ever. (58)

Some people, handsome by nature, have wilfully deformed
themselves. (1)

Beauty is dependence in the babe, a toothless, tender nurs-
ling;

Beauty is boldness in the boy, a curly, rosy truant;

Beauty is modesty and grace in fair, retiring girlhood. (62)

Beauty carries its dower in its face.

Beauty without grace is a violet without scent.

A strong and beautiful soul will show itself such, though
its body be feeble, sick, or ungraceful. (6)

In all that God hath made, in all that man hath marred,
lingereth beauty, or its wreck; a broken mould and castings.

And never yet hath lived the man, utterly beggared of the
beautiful.   (62)

Many hours wet and dull
Bring on an hour beautiful;
And thus it is that present gloom
Prepares a beauty that shall come.   (6)

She who is born a beauty is born betrothed.

Show me an enthusiast in aught; he hath noted one thing
narrowly; and lo! his keenness hath detected the one dear hiding-
place of beauty.   (62)

Eternal beauty, image fair, once stamped upon the soul,
before the eye all lovely stands, nor will depart; so God ordains.
(9)

Loveliness needs not the foreign aid of ornament,
But it is when unadorn'd adorn'd the most.   (5)

Affect not to despise beauty: no one is freed from its dominion;

But regard it not a pearl of price; it is fleeting as the bow
in the clouds.   (62)

What God hath made and meant to charm let not man
despise.   (62)

Beauty is openness and strength in pure high-minded youth;
man, the noble, and intelligent, gladdeneth earth in beauty; and
woman's beauty sunneth him, as with a smile from heaven.
(62)

Beauty, various in all things, setteth up her home in each
—shedding graciously around an omnipresent smile.   (62)

Fair tresses man's imperial race ensnare,
And beauty draws us with a single hair.   (2)

Albeit fairness in the creature shall often co-exist with ex-
cellence,

Yet hath many an angel shape been tenanted by fiends.
(62)

Dost thou nothing know of this, to be awed at woman's
beauty?   (62)

On Love, the Greatest Thing in the Universe.

O! quicker far is lover's ken
Than the dull glance of common men,
And, by strange sympathy, can spell
The thoughts the loved one will not tell   (29)

Love shall still be lord of all. (29)

Love betters what is best.
Lovers ever run before the clock.
       Love has no thought of self!
Love sacrifices all things to bless the thing it loves. (82)

Love hides even from itself. (64)

Love rules his kingdom without a sword
Love understands, and therefore waits (65)

The story without an end that angels throng to hear. (62)

There must be something somewhere that we cannot love too much. (155)

Love without return is like a question without an answer.
When one is truly in love, one not only says it, but shows it. (12)

Love is the true price at which love is bought.
All true love is grounded on esteem. (81)

To love is to be useful to yourself; to cause love is to be useful to others. (77)

Love is strong as death. (27)

Some persons, by hating vice too much, come to love men too little. (137)

There's a wideness in God's mercy like the wideness of the sea,

There is kindness in His justice which is more than liberty.
For the love of God is broader than the measure of man's mind,
And the heart of the Eternal is most wonderfully kind.
Love knows no limits.
God is love.
That "God is love" is not one side of the truth, but the whole truth about God—there is no other side. (154)

There is but one love in the universe. (161)

Love is not one of the attributes of God, but the sum of them all. (154)

Whether in its invisible source or in the faintest of its scattered beams love is essentially one thing. (155)

Nothing but love has ever reigned on the throne of creation; nothing but love ever will reign. (154)

The Lord appeared unto me, saying: "I have loved thee with an everlasting love; therefore, with loving kindness, have I drawn thee." (159)

> He prayeth well who loveth well both man and bird and
> beast;
> He prayeth best who loveth best all things both great and
> small,
> For the dear God, who loveth us, He made and loveth all.

Love is divine, but it is not exclusively divine . . . our very notion of the human heart is love; always and everywhere heart and love mean the same thing. (154)

Everyone that loveth is born of God. (157)

We shall never have to bide a greater weal or woe than the possession or the want of what we love. (155)

He that loveth not his brother whom he hath seen cannot love God whom he hath not seen. (157)

> I have heard of reasons manifold why love must needs be
> blind,
> But this the best of all I hold—His eyes are in his mind.
> (23)

As you give love, you will have love.
A loveless life is a living death.
> 'Tis better to have loved and lost,
> Than never to have loved at all. (124)

Love is not without its bitterness.
Love rules without a sword, and binds without a cord.
The strongest evidence of love is sacrifice. (155)

Love goes without that another may have. (154)

He that loveth not knoweth not God. (157)

Love casts its whole living into the treasury   it cannot keep its cruse of ointment; the instinct of its being is to give. Wherever you find love you find self-denial. (154)

He that loveth his neighbor hath fulfilled the law. (41)

Many waters cannot quench love, neither can the floods drown it; if a man would give all the substance of his house for love, it would be utterly contemned. (27)

If she cannot heal the scar, Love, at least will *hide*. (154)

Love covereth all transgressions. (27)

Love is of God. (157)

We love because He first loved us. (157)

Love walks backward with her mantle on her shoulders and covereth a multitude of sins. (154)

There is no fear in love, but perfect love casteth out fear. (157)

Love worketh no ill to his neighbor; love therefore is the fulfilment of the law. (41)

All goodness grows from love. (154)

This is my commandment, that ye love one another, even as I have loved you. Greater love hath no man than this: That a man lay down his life for his friends. (158)

I am persuaded that neither death, nor life, nor angels, nor principalities, nor things present, nor things to come, nor powers, nor height, nor depth, nor any other creature, shall be able to separate us from the love of God, which is in Christ Jesus our Lord. (41)

Surely it stands to reason that only a fuller love can compete with the love of the world. (65)

Justice is love's order. (154)

Let love be without hypocrisy. (160)

Who loves well is slow to forget.

They love us truly who correct us freely.

Love imputes no motives, sees the bright side, puts the best construction on every action. (65)

Those who have no money may have mercy. (21)

The merciful man doeth good to his own soul. (27)

True love never grows old.

Love is never satisfied with doing or giving anything but the best. (154)

Love is the rule for fulfilling all rules. (65)

Thy love to me was wonderful, passing the love of women. (156)

Love knows not labor.

Jacob served seven years for Rachel; and they seemed unto him but a few days, for the love he had to her.

To love and know in man is boundless appetite and boundless power, and these demonstrate boundless objects too. (8)

God will not love thee less because men love thee more. (62)

Love, I say, is energy of life. (53)

He that hath love in his breast hath spurs in his side.

Mother love is ever in its spring.

Rejoice in the wife of thy youth. . . . And be thou ravished always with her love. (27)

Do we not always grow to the likeness of what we love? (155)

There is a sweet and holy blindness in Christian love. (126)

Humble love,
And not proud reason, keeps the door of heaven;
Love finds admission where proud science fails. (8)

Love is the clue to human love;
Love is the clue to the love of God. (154)

Love is the fufilling of the law. (41)

Love and love only is the loan for love. (8)

Mercy and alms are the body and soul of charity. (21)

He who loves well obeys well.

Love knows hidden paths.

That is the best charity which so relieves another's poverty it still continues their industry. (1)

Charity cannot dwell with a mean and narrow spirit. (62)

That which is to be loved long is to be loved with reason rather than with passion. (79)

Works and not words, are the proof of love. (99)

In love is no lack.

Love makes the music of the blest above,
Heaven's harmony is universal love. (7)

Love doth ever shed rich healing where it nestles. (135)

Best is the man who would freely impart
    To a brother—whoever he be—
    Full worth for his work at the least;
That is, he should love all the good at his best
    And tenderly think of the bad
    (As we have spoken before);
The man he should love with his soul, for the rest
    His sins he should hate, and be glad
    To see them cut off evermore. (162)

Not God above gets all men's love. (160)

There is more pleasure in loving than in being beloved.

Love grows with obstacles.

Love can neither be bought nor sold; its only price is love.

Deeds are love and not fine phrases.

Love looketh softly from the eye and kindleth love by looking.

An honest love is not afraid to frown. (8)

Hail, Love! first Love, thou word that sums all bliss!
The sparkling cream of all Time's blessedness,
The silken down of happiness complete! (9)

Love's night is noon. (75)

Let not mercy and truth forsake thee, bind them about thy neck, write them upon the table of thine heart. (27)

Those whom love cements in holy faith, and equal transport, free as nature live, disdaining fear. (5)

Love has its instinct. (128)

Hail, holy Love! thou word that seems all bliss,
Gives and receives all bliss, fullest when most
Thou givest! spring-head of all felicity,
Deepest when most is drawn! emblem of God!
O'erflowing most when greatest numbers drink! (9)

Love levels all inequalities.

As love without esteem is capricious and volatile, esteem without love is languid and cold. (70)

Nothing is a hardship to love, and nothing is hard. (65)

Love in our hearts shall grow mighty and strong,
Through crosses, through sorrows, through manifold wrong.
                                   (12)

Where there is great love there is great pain.

How in the turmoil of life can love stand, where there is not one heart and one mouth and one hand?   (12)

Love demands faith and faith firmness.

To love for the pure sake of loving is almost the characteristic of an angel.   (117)

Love will creep where it cannot go.

Charity is praised of all, and fear not thou that praise.
(62)

Charity walketh with a high step and stumbleth not at a trifle.   (62)

Love rules without law.

Charity hath keen eyes, but the lashes half conceal them.
(62)

Who love too much hate in the same extreme.   (2)

Love makes us like.   (123)

The heart whose hidden store is most has freest gift for all mankind.   (6)

On Speech and Silence; or the Tongue
Untamed and Civilized.

It has been said: "Speech is silvern and silence is golden." I have known them both when they have been wooden.   (161)

The noblest of all forms of government is self-government, but it is the most difficult.   (262)

Speak clearly if you speak at all;
Carve every word before you let it fall.   (176)

In peopled cities, as in waste untrod,
Its tones are mighty—'tis the voice of God.   (175)

Silence is the perfectest herald of joy. I were but little happy if I could say how much.   (32)

Speech ventilates our intellectual fire.   (8)

The fool shineth no longer than he holdeth his tongue.

A tattler is worse than a thief.

The tongue can no man tame: it is a restless evil—full of deadly poison.   (165)

No one ever repented of having held his tongue.

The tongue is a little member and boasteth great things.
(165)

How oftentimes is silence the wisest of replies. (62)

The tongue is not steel—yet it cuts.
Well-timed silence hath more eloquence than speech. (62)

Whoso keepeth his mouth and his tongue, keepeth his soul from troubles. (27)

The tongue breaketh bone, though itself have none.
Give your tongue more holiday than your hands or eyes.
(89)

Death and life are in the power of the tongue. (27)

Give thy thoughts no tongue,
Nor any unproportioned thought his act. (32)

Silence is an excellent remedy against slander. (21)

Silence answers much.
Who has not a good tongue ought to have good hands.
A lying tongue is but for a moment. (27)

Good silence is near holiness.
A slip of the foot may be soon recovered, but that of the tongue perhaps never.

There is that speaketh rashly like the piercings of a sword; but the tongue of the wise is health. (27)

Give every man thine ear, but few thy voice:
Take each man's censure, but reserve thy judgment. (32)

He that hath a perverse tongue falleth into mischief. (27)

The tongue talks at the head's cost.
A silent man's words are not brought into court.
The long unanswered letter doth friendship nigh to death,
And few affections can endure determined dogged silence.
(62)

He knows much who knows how to hold his tongue.
A fair face will get its praise, though the owner keep silent.
There were no ill language were it not ill taken.
The tongue of the righteous is as choice silver. (27)

Health can hear therein only glad hopes and memories,
While nervous irritable diseases hath peopled it with fears.
(62)

Many have fallen by the edge of the sword, but not so many as have fallen by the tongue. (10)

That by well-doing ye should put to silence the ignorance of foolish men; so is the will of God.   (166)

In the company of strangers silence is safe.
The froward tongue shall be cut out.   (27)

Thistles and thorns prick sore, but evil tongues prick more.
More have repented of speech than silence.
The tongue wounds more than a lance.
Silence is the best reply to the ignorant.   (75)

A great talker is a great liar.
He who would close another man's mouth should first tie up his own.
Thou shalt be hid from the scourge of the tongue.   (164)
Turn your tongue seven times before talking.
Who can estimate the torments worked by tongue and temper,
Those dislocations on the rack, of comfort and of love.
(62)

Be checked for silence,
But never tax'd for speech.   (32)

He that can rule his tongue shall live without strife.   (10)

Woe for the misery and crime an aggravating tongue can cause!   (62)

A flow of words is no proof of wisdom.
When a tell-tale might do harm, be sure it is prudent to be dumb.   (62)

He who says what he likes, must hear what he does not like.
Silence seldom doth harm.

In the cause of good be wise, and in a case indifferent, keep silence.   (62)

We ought either to be silent or to speak things that are better than silence.   (163)

The worst wheel of a cart creaks most.
Silence is less injurious than a bad reply.   (42)

Nature has given us two ears, two eyes, and but one tongue, to the end we should hear and see more than we speak.   (167)

A wise man tighteneth his tongue, speaking less than thinking.   (62)

There is a knack of showing we understand the matter,
when we hold our peace.

The keen mind, full of thought, rejoiceth in a quiet hour.

While dullards hold it irksome, to be killed as best they
can. (62)

Rehearse not unto another that which is told unto thee, and
thou shalt fare never the worse. (10)

So too, when many praise, as well as when they blame,
And when thy name is loudest in the mouths of men,
Thy strength is to sit still, in wise and humble silence;
Let Silence lay her finger on thine unpresumptuous lip.
(62)

Let thy speech be short, comprehending much in few
words; be as one that knoweth and yet holdeth his tongue.
(10)

Whoso keepeth his mouth and his tongue, keepeth his soul
from troubles. (27)

And woe, too, for the clamorous home where silence hath no
lover,
But scolding worry drowneth good, alike by day and night.
(62)

One man may teach another to speak; but none can teach
another to hold his peace. (9)

Neither speak well nor ill of yourself. If well, men will not
believe you; if ill, they will believe a great deal more than
you say.

When insolence provoketh, when slander false accuseth,
When ignorance, and prejudice are full of idle talk,
Let silence be the answer on thy lip and in thy life. (62)

He that would love life and see good days, let him refrain
his tongue from evil and his lips that they speak no guile. (166)

Silently as a dream. (7)

Silent as the grave. (179)

Silent as a standing pool. (85)

Silent as thought. (177)

Silent as the night. (180)

Silent as falling dews. (181)

Silent as the foot of time. (178)

34

Silent as the growth of flowers. (182)

Silent as your shadow. (183)

Silent as snow falls on the earth. (184)

As silent as the day gives away to night. (185)

A man of silence is a man of sense.

A bridle for the tongue is a fine piece of harness.

If you don't say it, you'll not have to unsay it.

He talks much who has least to say.

He cannot speak well who cannot hold his tongue.

If wisdom's ways you wisely seek, five things observe with
    care:

Of whom you speak, to whom you speak, and how, and
    when, and where.

Talking comes by nature, silence by wisdom.

A tame tongue is a rare bird.

On Conscience.

A good conscience is a soft pillow.

He that loses his conscience has nothing left that is worth
keeping. (216)

A quiet conscience sleeps in thunder.

A good conscience needs never sneak.

A clear conscience can bear any trouble.

A wounded conscience is able to unparadise Paradise itself. (1)

A good conscience is the best divinity.

The worst man is least troubled by his conscience. (123)

One self-approving hour whole years outweighs. (2)

Conscience makes cowards of us all. (32)

An evil conscience is always fearful and unquiet. (18)

A good conscience is a choice companion.

A guilty conscience needs no accusing.

My dominion ends where that of conscience begins. (174)

Galled horses can't endure the comb.

I feel within me a peace above all earthly dignities—

A still and quiet conscience. (32)

Thou shalt rest sweetly if they heart condemn thee not.

(18)

Hearken to the warnings of conscience, if you would not feel its wounds.

The glory of the good is in their consciences, and not in the tongues of men. (18)

On Health, Happiness and Holiness.

Blessed is the peacemaker, not the conqueror.
Holiness—the livery of the soldiery of God. (9)

You must not pledge your own health.

The best physicians are Dr. Diet, Dr. Quiet, and Dr. Merryman.

There is no riches above a sound body, and no joy above the joy of the heart. (10)

The surest guide to health, say what they will, is never
to suppose we shall be ill;
Most of those evils we poor mortals know, from doctors and
imagination flow. (188)

If you be not ill, be not ill-like. (69)

Guard good health from heat, and cold, and wet, and sudden
changes;
A little care, a little sense, shall save thee bitter trouble;
It is no petty moral to preserve thy body's health. (62)

A sound mind in a sound body, is the blessedness of
creatures;
So spake the wise of old, and we cannot mend their wisdom.

Blessed is the man that walketh not in the counsel of the ungodly, nor standeth in the way of sinners, nor sitteth in the seat of the scornful. (156)

The gladness of the heart is the life of a man. (10)

Blessed is the man unto whom the Lord imputeth not inquity, and in whose spirit there is no guile. (156)

The more we limit and concentrate happiness, the more certain we are of securing it. (86)

Blessed is he whose transgression is forgiven, whose sin is covered. (156)

The happy only are truly great. (8)

Happy is he that hath the God of Jacob for his help. (156)

True happiness has no localities,
No tones provincial, no peculiar garb. (9)

Happy is the man that findeth wisdom . . . . and everyone that retaineth her. (27)

Joy is an import; joy is an exchange; Joy flies monopolists; it calls for two. (8)

He that hath mercy on the poor—happy is he. (27)

The day returns and brings us the petty round of irritating concerns and duties. Help us to play the man, help us to perform them with laughter and kind faces, let cheerfulness abound with industry. Give us to go blithely on our business this day, bring us to our resting beds weary and content and undishonored, and grant us in the end the gift of sleep. (260)

How happy is he, born or taught, that serveth not another's will,
Whose armor is his honest thought, and simple truth his utmost skill. (189)

Blessed are the undefiled in the way—who walk in the law of the Lord. (158)

Much joy not only speaks small happiness,
But happiness that shortly must expire. (8)

Blessed are the poor in spirit: for theirs is the Kingdom of Heaven. (158)

Happiness consists in the multiplicity of agreeable consciousness. (79)

Blessed are they that mourn: for they shall be comforted. (158)

Thes common course of things is in favor of happiness; happiness is the *rule,* misery the *exception.* (190)

Blessed are they which do hunger and thirst after righteousness: for they shall be filled. (158)

What does the man who transient joys prefers?
What, but prefer the bubbles to the stream. (8)

Blessed are the merciful: for they shall obtain mercy. (158)

Domestic happiness, thou only bliss
Of Paradise that has survived the fall! (7)

Blessed are the pure in heart: for they shall see God. (158)

Holiness is the regeneration of innocence. (6)

There is in man a higher thought than love of happiness; he can do without happiness, and instead thereof find blessedness. (33)

Blessed are they that hear the word of God, and keep it. (186)

Blessed are they that have not seen, and yet have believed. (158)

Blessed are the meek: for they shall inherit the earth. (158)

Blessed are the dead which die in the Lord. (157)

The great lesson to be learned is that Happiness is within us. No passing amusement, no companionship, no material possession can permanently satisfy. We must hoard up our own Strength. We must depend upon our own Resources for amusement and pleasure. We must make or mar our own Tranquillity. To teach them this is the preparation for Life which we can give our children. (267)

We cannot find happiness until we forget to seek for it. We cannot find Peace until we enter the Path of Self-sacrificing Usefulness. (266)

Blessed are they which are persecuted for righteousness' sake: for theirs is the Kingdom of Heaven. (158)

Blessed is the man that endureth temptation. (165)

Blessed are the peacemakers: for they shall be called the children of God. (158)

No man e'er found a happy life by chance,
Or yawn'd it into being with a wish;
Or with the snout of grov'ling appetite
E'er smelt it out, and grubb'd it from the dirt—
And art it is, and must be learnt; and learnt
With unremitting effort, or be lost. (8)

Happiness is unrepented pleasure. (167)

Happiness is no other than soundness and perfection of mind. (97)

Were all men happy, revellings would cease. (8)

I love such mirth as does not make friends ashamed to look upon one another next morning. (118)

Happiness depends, as Nature shows,
Less on exterior things than most suppose. (7)

But where to find that happiest spot below
Who can direct, when all pretend to know? (3)

Joy surfeited turns to sorrow.
Joys shared with others are more enjoyed.
True happiness ne'er entered at an eye.
True happiness resides in things unseen. (8)

All who joy would win
Must share it—Happiness was born a twin. (168)

Every life has its joy; every joy its law.
May heav'n ne'er trust my friend with happiness
Till it has taught him how to bear it well
By previous pain; and made it safe to smile! (8)

The mind that would be happy must be great:
Great in its wishes; great in its surveys:
Extended views a narrow mind extend. (8)

He is the happy man whose life e'en now
Shows somewhat of that happier life to come. (7)

Every freeman should seek till he find
That, which I spake of,—good—endless in worth:
These, which I sing of,—the joys of the mind. (162)

Mind is a kingdom to the man who gathereth his pleasure
from Ideas. (62)

How distant oft the thing we doat on most
From that for which we doat, felicity! (8)

The song of mirth is soon past, for happiness counts not
the hours. (9)

If bliss had lien in art or strength,
None but the wise or strong had gained it. (4)

A perpetuity of bliss is bliss. (8)

True happiness is to no place confined,
But still is found with a contented mind.
Bliss is too great to lodge within an hour—
Duration is essential to the name. (8)

On Children.

Better their laughter than a chamber neat.
Only in their mirth is home complete.   (63)

Children are what the mothers are.   (76)

He who takes the child by the hand takes the mother by the heart.
Children are what they are made.
Children are certain cares, but uncertain comforts.
A tender nest of soft young hearts, each to be separately
studied,
A curious eager flock of minds to be severally tamed and
tutored.   (62)

Mothers may have illegitimate children, but fathers simply
have natural sons.   (257)

What is learned in the cradle lasts till the grave.
What the child hears at the fireside is soon known at the
parish church.
A wise son maketh a glad father, but a foolish son is the
heaviness of his mother.   (27)

Let a child have its will and it will not cry.
Chastise a good child that it may not grow bad, and a bad,
one that it may not grow worse.
A colt you may break, but an old horse you never can.
The friendship of a child is the brightest gem set upon the
circlet of Society.
A jewel worth a world of pains—a jewel seldom seen.   (62)

He will not blush that has a father's heart
To take in childish plays a childish part;
    But bends his sturdy back to any toy
That youth takes pleasure in to please his boy.   (7)

Delightful task! to rear the tender thought,
To teach the young idea how to shoot,
To pour the fresh instruction o'er the mind,
To breathe th' enlivening spirit, and to fix
The generous purpose in the glowing breast.   (5)

' Suffer the little children, and forbid them not to come unto
me; for of such is the kingdom of Heaven.   (158)

40

Except ye turn, and become as little children, ye shall in no wise enter into the kingdom of Heaven. (158)

Ye are of God, little children, and have overcome: because greater is He that is in you than he that is in the world. (157)

On Friendship.

A friend is worth all hazards we can run. (8)

A good friend is one's nearest relation.

A man that hath friends must show himself friendly. (27)

Our worst enemies are the friends who have failed to find us profitable.

There is no better looking-glass than an old friend.

A man may travel through the world and sow it thick with friendships. (62)

The best way to represent to life the manifold uses of friendship, is to cast and see how many things one cannot do for one's self. (19)

Promises may get friends, but 'tis performances that keep them.

A friend loveth at all times. (27)

You will never have a friend if you must have one without fault.

Friendships multiply joys and divide griefs.

Adversity is the only balance to weigh friends. (94)

Every man is a friend to him that giveth gifts. (27)

A friend to everybody is a friend to nobody.

True friends visit us in prosperity only when invited, but in adversity they come without invitation. (171)

Judge before friendship, then confide till death. (8)

Thine own friend and thy father's friend forsake not. (27)

Better friends can no man have than those whom God hath given.

And he that hath despised the gift, thought ill of that he knew not. (62)

A friend's faults may be noticed, but not blamed.

Faithful are the wounds of a friend. (27)

41

A friend that you buy with presents will be bought from you.

He is my friend that helps me, and not he that pities me.

A hedge between keeps friendship green.

Iron sharpeneth iron, so a man sharpeneth the countenance of his friend. (27)

No face is ever hopelessly plain through which a friendly soul looks out upon the world.

Reserve will wound it, and distrust destroy. (8)

To be honest, to be kind, to earn a little, to spend a little less, to renounce whatever shall be necessary and not be embittered, to make a family happier for his presence, to keep a few friends and these without capitulation, and above all, to keep friends with one's self—here is a task for all that a man has of fortitude and delicacy. (260)

Friendship's the wine of life; but friendship new is neither strong nor pure. (8)

There is a friend that sticketh closer than any brother. (27)

A true friend does sometimes venture to be offensive.

Common friendship standeth on equalities, and cannot bear a debt. (62)

He that ceaseth to be a friend never was a good one.

The rich hath many friends. (27)

Absence strengtheneth friendship, where the last recollections were kindly.

A mountain is made up of atoms, and friendship of little matters; and if atoms hold not together the mountain is crumbled into dust. (62)

Make no friendship with a man given to anger. (27)

Hope not to find a friend, but what has found a friend in
   thee,
All like the purchase, few the price will pay,
And this makes friends such miracles below. (8)

Heaven gives us friends, to bless the present scene;
Resumes them to prepare us for the next. (8)

Wealth addeth many friends. (27)

The friends thou hast, and their adoption tried,
Grapple them to thy soul with hooks of steel;

But do not dull thy palm with entertainment
Of each new-hatch'd unfledged comrade. (32)

Know ye not that the friendship of the world is enmity with
God? (165)

No friendship will abide the test,
That stands on sordid interest . . .
Who seeks a friend should come, dispos'd
To exhibit, in full bloom disclos'd,
    The graces and the beauties
That form the character he seeks.

    . . . . . .

An envious man, if you succeed,
May prove a dangerous foe indeed,
    But not a friend worth keeping.
Beware no negligence of yours,
Such as a friend but ill endures
    Enfeeble his affection.
The man that hails you "Tom!" or "Jack!"
And proves by thumps upon your back
    How he esteems your merit,
Is such a friend that one had need
Be very much his friend indeed
    To pardon or to bear it.

The noblest friendship ever shown
The Saviour's history makes known.

Friendship made in a moment is of no moment.
False friends are worse than open enemies.
Choose your friends with care, that you may have choice
friends.
A good friend is better than a near relation.
A faithful friend loves to the end.
He is a weak friend who cannot bear with his friend's
weakness.
A friend is easier lost than found.

On Faults and What to Do With Them
When They are Found.

You would spy faults if your eyes were out.
Conceal defects for charity, and cover up small faults.

            (62)

A fault once denied is twice committed.

We get just anything we prepare for, and nothing else. Everything that happens is a sequence: this happened today because you did that yesterday. (257)

Where love fails we espy all faults.

What glory is it, if, when ye be buffeted for your faults, ye shall take it patiently? (166)

In other men we faults can spy,
And blame the mote that dims their eye;
Each little speck and blemish find—
To our own stronger errors blind. (72)

Forget others' faults by remembering your own.
Confess your faults one to another. (165)

If a man be overtaken in a fault, ye who are spiritual restore such an one in a spirit of meekness, considering thyself, lest thou also be tempted. (41)

Faults in the life breed errors in the brain,
And these reciprocally those again. (7)

Denying a fault doubles it.
He that confesseth his fault shall be preserved from hurt. (10)

A subject's faults a subject may proclaim,
A monarch's errors are forbidden game! (7)

Where there is no love, all are faults.

If thy brother sin against thee, go, shew him his fault between thee and him alone. (158)

Not to repent of a fault is to justify it.

If the best man's faults were written on his forehead, it would make him pull his hat over his eyes. (71)

Whoever thinks a faultless piece to see,
Thinks what ne'er was, nor is, nor e'er shall be. (2)

Cleanse thou me from secret faults. (156)

They are without fault before the throne of God. (157)

Now unto Him that is able to . . . . present you faultless before the presence of His glory with exceeding joy. (173)

A fault confessed is half redressed.

If love finds fault, it is that fault may not be found by others.

Any thing, any institution, or any one not well enough put together to stand the racket of Life should die—and does. (257)

It is quite absurd to say that a man is good or bad—he is good and bad. (257)

Every man has his little weakness. It often takes the form of a desire to get something for nothing. (257)

A fault-mender is better than a fault-finder.

> Many find fault without any end,
> And yet do nothing at all to mend.

Few are the faults we flatter when alone. (8)

He has bad food who feeds on others' faults.

> However blind a man may be,
> Another's faults he's sure to see.

Most people will sooner be told their fortunes than their faults.

Thoughts for the Thirsty.

Whiskey!—it dragged Edgar Allan Poe from the starlit heights where he penned "El Dorado" and "For Annie" down to the Baltimore gutter from which he was picked up dying. (273)

Many a child is thungry because the brewer is rich.

"Another pot!" Try the tea-pot.

Where there is drink there is danger.

Be not drunk with wine. (41)

Beer is never so flat as those who drink it.

Whiskey drinking is risky drinking.

Who hath woe? Who hath sorrow? Who hath contentions? Who hath babbling? Who hath wounds without a cause? Who hath redness of eyes? They that tarry long at the wine; they that go to seek mixed wine. (27)

Don't let the public-house live on your private house.

Drink first dims, then darkens, then deadens, then damns.

Drink like a fish—water only.

> He who often hugs the pewter,
> Sure his thirst becomes acuter.

If you get the best of whiskey, it will get the best of you.

The misfortune of those who are advocating prohibitory laws, whether they are to be applied to Sunday or week-day usages, is that in their zeal for one object, and that a very good object, they fail to recognize the influence of their methods upon the minds of those who look at a subject less microscopically and more widely and largely than they do. (263)

The best side of a saloon is the outside.

Be not among wine-bibbers! (27)

The priest and the prophet who have erred through strong drink—they are swallowed up of wine; they are out of the way through strong drink; they err in vision; they stumble in judgment. (186)

Keep your lip from sip and sip.

No man is made top-heavy by a pull at the pump.

Take the pledge and "pledge" no more.

Water is a strong drink; Samson drank it.

Liquor talks mighty loud when it gets out of the jug.

Stout makes many lean.

Leave the brown October (ale), and keep yourself sober.

When women consume gin, gin soon consumes them.

Ardent spirits are evil spirits.

Don't make your nose blush for the sins of your mouth.

Better wear the blue than bear the blues.

If I drink beer, it makes me queer.

Counsels that are given in wine.
    Will do no good to thee or thine.

Beer brings many to their bier.

A drinking dame—a sight of shame!

No sane man can be in any doubt about the enormous dangers to our modern life of the drink habit.

Adam's ale is the best brew.

The tankard is the greatest thief.

Mind that *porter* does not carry you off.

Be in good spirits without ardent spirits.

The ale-jug is a great waster.

    Bacchus well his sheep he knows!
    For he marks them on the nose.

He who considers all lets the wine-cup fall.

The quart pot helpeth not.

Who drinketh wine, his nose will shine.

If Jack drinks the wages, Jill cannot save them.

Some earn a dime and get a dollar's worth of thirst.

Satan's palace—the gin palace.

Put glasses to thine eyes, not to thy lips.

A drunkard's mouth dries up his pocket.

Don't color your nose with saloon-keepers' paint.

First the distiller, then the doctor, then the undertaker.

Some drink healths till they drink away their own health.

No gifts on earth pure water can excel;
Nature's the brewer, and she brews it well.

Men are strong and hale without strong ale.

Keep far from the bar and the barrel.

Grape-juice kills more than grape-shot.

A drop of gin is a drop too much.

The home may soon be full of gear,
If you will learn to save the beer.

Purses shrink while workmen drink.

If men would think they'd give up drink.

Liquor very loudly talks when the screw has drawn the corks.

He will never drink too much who never drinks at all.

Drink won't hurt you if you don't drink it.

Cans of beer cost many a tear.

"Something short"—a drunkard's sense.

Blue ribbon is better than blue ruin.

Good wine ruins the purse, and bad wine ruins the stomach.

Drinking and stuffing makes a man a ragamuffin.

The best medicine is temperance.

Strong drink is the devil's way to man, and man's way to the devil.

Drink injures a man externally, internally and eternally.

The bottle and the glass make many cry "Alas!"

Drink no wine and you'll not drink too much.

Wine is a mocker, strong drink is raging; and whosoever is deceived thereby is not wise. (27)

Drunkenness turns a man out of himself, and leaves a beast in his room.

Look not thou upon the wine when it is red; when it giveth his color in the cup; when it moveth itself aright. At the last it biteth like a serpent and stingeth like an adder. (27)

Voluntary total abstinence must always be the only safe rule with many men. Enforced total abstinence has been in America the parent of immeasurable dishonesty and hypocrisy. (263)

Whiskey is very harmless—if you don't drink it.
There is a devil in every berry of the grape. (187)
Wine hath drowned more men than the sea.
The drunkard continually assaults his own life.

On Anger, Folly, Falsehood, Flattery, and Treachery.

Anger manages everything badly. (93)

A boaster and a fool are two of a school.

A fool is fond of writing his name where it should not be.

A wilful falsehood told is a cripple, not able to stand by itself without some one to support it. (1)

There is no such flatterer as a man's self.

The treason pleases—but not the traitor.

> When I see a person's name
> Scratched upon a glass.
> I know he owns a diamond,
> And his father owns an ass.

An angry man opens his mouth and shuts his eyes.

He who will be angry for anything will be angry for nothing.
(1)

Anger and haste hinder good counsel.

Anger may glance into the breast of a wise man, but rests only in the bosom of fools.

Though very troublesome to others, anger is most so to him that has it. (21)

Anger punishes itself.

The end of wrath is the beginning of repentance.

Angry words fan the fire like wind. (21)

Whosoever is angry with his brother shall be in danger of the judgment. (158)

Wrath avoideth no quarrel. (62)

Whate'er's begun in anger ends in shame.

> Be not quick to take offense:
> Anger is a foe to sense.

Grow angry slowly; there's plenty of time.

An angry man is a man in a fever.

> Madness and anger differ but in this—
> This is short madness, that long anger is.

He that is angry is seldom at ease.

Be not hasty in thy spirit to be angry: for anger resteth in the bosom of fools. (192)

Cease from anger and forsake wrath. (156)

Anger begins with folly and ends with repentance.

Anger is often more hurtful than the injury that caused it.

When you die your trumpeter will be buried.

God and men think him a fool who brags of his own wisdom.

> Oh that the tongue would quiet stay,
> And let the hand its power display!

A boaster and a liar are much about the same thing.

Little bantams are great at crowing.

One penny in the pot (money-box) makes more noise than when it is full.

Folly taxes us four times as much as Congress.

Stripes are prepared for the back of fools. (27)

A great man's foolish sayings pass for wise ones.

Fools grow without watering.

Fools live but do not learn.

Fools make those inquiries afterwards which wise men make before.

Fools' names you see on seat and tree.

Shame shall be the promotion of fools. (27)

It is folly's most peculiar attribute and native act to make experience void. (9)

Fools rush in where angels fear to tread. (2)

A fool must now and then be right—by chance. (7)

No folly keeps its color in death's sight. (8)

A fool loseth his estate before he finds his folly.

Answer not a fool according to his folly, lest thou also be like unto him. (27)

A fool uttereth all his mind. (27)

Hope and expectation are a fool's income.

The way of a fool is right in his own eyes. (27)

A prating fool shall fall. (28)

The follies none are found to praise, let them die unblamed.

(62)

The fool hath said in his heart, There is no God.   (156)
A fool and his money are soon parted.
A fool's fortune is his misfortune.
A fool says, "I can't;" a wise man says, "I'll try."
A fool is never wrong.
A fool is a man who is wise too late.
A fool lingers long, but time hurries on.
A fool in his own house will not be wise in mine.
A fool in a gown is none the wiser.
A man may be a fool and not know it.
A foolish man diligently advertises his own folly.
A foolish man is generally a proud man.
If every fool were crowned, the majority of the population would be kings.
If every unwise man died, no one would be buried—there would be no one to dig a grave.
An easy fool is a knave's tool.
If there were no fools there would be no war.
Men may live fools, but fools they cannot die.   (8)

> That man most justly fool I call,
> Who takes to scribbling on a wall.

A lie begets a lie till they come to generations.

> A whispered lie is just as wrong
> As one that thunders loud and long.

A lie is a foul blot in a man.   (10)
Liars begin by imposing upon others, but end by deceiving themselves.
It is easy to tell a lie, hard to tell but a lie.   (1)
A liar is a bravo towards God and a coward towards men.
(19)

Credit won by lying is quick in dying.

> Oh, what a tangled web we weave,
> When first we practice to deceive!   (29)

A false witness shall not be unpunished.   (27)
A liar giveth ear to a naughty tongue.   (27)
Falseness often lurks beneath fair hair.
Thou shalt not bear false witness against thy neighbor.
(191)

A poor man is better than a liar.
A false witness shall perish.   (27)

Falsehood follows at the heels of debt.

Beads about the neck and the devil in the heart.

The lie that flatters I abhor the most.   (7)

A flattering mouth worketh ruin.   (27)

Flattery is like friendship in show, but not in fruit.   (167)

Flattery fouls the flatterer and the flattered.

> If others say how good are you,
> Ask yourself if it is true.

A man that flattereth his neighbor spreadeth a net for his feet.   (27)

The idol rejoiceth in his incense, and loveth not to shame his suppliants; should he seek to find them false, his honors die with theirs.   (62)

> Treason doth never prosper: what's the reason?
> For if it prosper none dare call it treason.

Judas, dost thou betray me with a kiss?

> Canst thou find hell about my lips?—and miss
> Of life, just at the gates of life and bliss?   (4)

On the Worst Foes of Mankind: Envy, Hatred, Malice, Pride, Arrogance, Cruelty, Jealousy, Suspicion, Hypocrisy.

Envy shoots at others, but hits itself.

Who is able to stand before envy?   (27)

The greatest mischief you can do the envious, is to do well.

Envy is a moth to the heart, a canker to the thought, and a rust to the soul.   (217)

Envy is the rottenness of the bones.   (27)

> Base envy withers at another's joy,
> And hates that excellence it cannot reach.   (5)

Envy is blind, and has no other quality but that of detracting from virtue.   (108)

Envy slayeth the silly ones.   (164)

Harbor not that vice called envy, lest another's happiness be your torment.

> Pride poisoned with malice becomes envy.
> There are better ways of showing your sand than throwing grit in the other man's eyes.
> What makes the man of envy what he is
> Is—worth in others, vileness in himself,

A lust of praise, with undeserving deeds
And conscious poverty of soul. (9)

No one would be envied if his whole estate were known.
(62)

Envy will merit, as its shade, pursue;
But, like a shadow, proves the substance true. (2)

No enmity so hard and fierce that kindness cannot melt.
(62)

He who wronged you will hate you.

The hatred of those who are most nearly connected is the most inveterate. (194)

Hate furroweth the brow, and a man may frown till he hateth. (62)

They that hate the righteous shall be desolate. (156)

Hatred stirreth up strife. (27)

He that would hate in the deep of his heart
Another,—unrighteous is he,
And worse than a bird or a beast. (162)

Hatred is as blind as love.

Willing to wound, and yet afraid to strike,
Just hint a fault, and hesitate dislike. (32)

Malice drinketh its own poison.

Malice hath a sharp sight and a strong memory.

Injury is to be measured by malice.

Malice is mindful.

They who are often at the looking-glass seldom spin.

A proud man hath many crosses.

A proud look makes foul work in a fine face.

Pride goeth before destruction, and a haughty spirit before a fall. (27)

He who swells in prosperity will shrink in adversity.

One friendly recognition, some passing words of kindness,
Would break the arctic circle that estrangeth class from class:
Yet neighbor meeteth neighbor ungreeted year by year,
And high and low, and all between them crystallize apart.
(62)

Pride is not more sinful than it is dangerous. (21)

Scorn the proud man that is ashamed to weep. (8)

Pride, self-adoring pride, is primal cause
Of all sin past, all pain, all woe to come.   (9)

Pride frustrates its own desire; it will not mount the steps of the throne, because it has not yet the crown on.   (6)

The proud are always most provoked by pride.   (7)

    A proud heart in a poor breast
    Gives its owner little rest.

By pride cometh contention.   (27)

When pride cometh, then cometh destruction.   (27)

There never was a looking-glass that told a woman she was ugly.

A proud man is always a foolish man.

The nobler the blood the less the pride.

Pride ne'er leaves its master till he gets a fa'.   (69)

Pride an' grace ne'er dwell in ae place.   (69)

Pride will not act unless it be allowed that it can succeed; and it will do nothing rather than not do it brilliantly.   (6)

Pride would be acknowledged victor before it has won the battle.   (**6**)

    Of all the causes which conspire to blind
    Man's erring judgment, and misguide the mind,
    What the weak head with strongest bias rules,
    Is pride, the never-failing vice of fools.   (2)

Arrogance is the obstruction of wisdom.

Arrogance is a weed that grows mostly on a dunghill.

If in thine own home, a cautious man and captious,

Thou hintest at suspicion of a servant, thou soon wilt make a thief.   (**62**)

He that will not be merciful to his beast is a beast himself.
(1)

A man of cruelty is God's enemy.

The jealous housewife is affection's direst foe.   (62)

Love being jealous makes a good eye look asquint.

Jealousy counteth its suspicions.   (62)

Jealousy is cruel as the grave.   (27)

It is as hard for the good to suspect evil as it is for the bad to suspect good.   (193)

When mistrust enters, love departs.

A slight suspicion may destroy a good repute.

If thou observest upon friends, as seeking thee selfishly for interest,

Thou hast hurt their kindliness to thee, and shalt be paid with scorn. (62)

In an atmosphere of suspicion men shrivel up. (65)

Be ever vigilant, but never suspicious.

If, too keen in care, thou dost *evidently* disbelieve thy child,

Thou hast injured the texture of his honor, and smoothed to him the way of lying. (62)

The hypocrite's hope shall perish. (164)

A hypocrite with his mouth destroyeth his neighbor. (27)

The hypocrite has meikle prayer but little devotion. (69)

If thou wilt think evil of thy neighbor, soon shalt thou have him for thy foe;

And yet he may know nothing of the cause that maketh thee distasteful to his soul;—

The cause of unkind suspicion, for which thou hast thy punishment. (62)

The hypocrite steals the livery of the court of heaven to serve the devil in. (9)

What is the hope of the hypocrite though he hath gained? (164)

I can smile, and murder while I smile;
And cry content to that which grieves my heart;
And wet my cheeks with artificial tears;
And frame my face to all occasions. (32)

Hypocrisy is the homage which vice pays to virtue. (209)

Trust not him that seems a saint. (1)

Neither man nor angel can discern
Hypocrisy, the only evil that walks
Invisible, except to God alone. (26)

We'll mock the time with fairest show;
The face must hide what the false heart doth know. (32)

He hath put forth his hands against such as be at peace with him; he hath broken his covenant; the words of his mouth were smoother than butter, but war was in his heart; his words were softer than oil, yet they were drawn swords. (156)

Hypocrisy is the necessary burden of villainy. (79)

I clothe my naked villainy
With odd ends, stol'n forth of Holy Writ;
And seem a saint, when most I play the devil. (32)

On Yesterday, To-day and To-morrow.

Water run by will not turn a mill.

We cannot erase the sad records from our past. (123)

Nor the good ones either, thank God. (161)

But will it mend the road before
To grieve for that behind? (63)

The time will come when winter will ask us: What were you doing all the summer? (195)

Past hours, if not by guilt, yet wound us by their flight. (8)

Forget your past circumstances, whether they be sorrows or joys. The one is not without remedy, the other not perfect. Both are past; why remember them? (123)

There is a past which is gone for ever; but there is a future which is still our own.

Time in advance, behind him hides his wings,
And seems to creep decrepit with his age;
Behold him when past by; what then is seen
But his broad pinions swifter than the winds? (8)

To-day is yesterday's pupil.

One to-day is worth two to-morrows.

Take time by the forelock.

By losing present time we lose all time.

Then time turns torment, when man turns fool. (8)

Be always in time: too late is a crime.

Tho' much and warm the wise have urg'd; the man
Is yet unborn, who duly weighs an hour. (8)

Give thy purse rather than thy time.

A man who does nothing never has time to do anything.

Any time means no time.

The idle call is a heavy tax where time is counted gold.
(62)

Each moment on the former shuts the grave. (8)

The greatest expense we can be at is that of our time.
A wise man redeemeth his time that he may improve his chances. (62)

To-day gold—to-morrow dust.
We take no note of time
But from its loss: to give it then a tongue
Is wise in man. (8)

They who make the best use of their time have none to spare.
If trifling kills,
Sure vice must butcher. O what heaps of slain
Cry out for vengeance on us! Time destroyed
Is suicide, where more than blood is spilt. (8)

Lost time is never found again.
The time that bears no fruit deserves no name. (8)

He that has most time has none to lose.
Nothing is more precious than time, yet nothing less valued.
Man flees from time, and time from man, too soon
In sad divorce this double flight must end. (8)

What greater crime than loss of time?
Money is not gained by losing time.
In the short life of man no lost time can be afforded.
We waste, not use our time: we breathe, not live.
Time wasted is existence; us'd is life. (8)

"More time!" is the usual exclamation, even by those who have all the time there is. They should bethink themselves about "more method," or else waste less time. (161)

Joy and sorrow are to-day and to-morrow.
Lose no time; be always employed in something useful. Keep out of all unnecessary action. (14)

If men strive together, and one smite another with a stone, or with his fist, and he die not, but keepeth his bed; if he rise again, and walk abroad upon his staff, then shall he that smote him be quit: only he shall pay for the loss of his time. (191)

Take time when time is—for time will away.
To let time slip is a reverseless crime:
You may have time again, but not *the* time. (196)

Now is now-here, but to-morrow's no-where.

Strength for to-day is all we need,
    For there never will be a to-morrow;
For to-morrow will prove but another to-day
    With its measure of joy and of sorrow.
Often the precious present is wasted in visions of the future.
                                                            (62)

If you won't do better to-day, you'll do worse to-morrow.
Often, the painful present is comforted by flattering the
    future,
And kind to-morrow beareth half the burdens of to-day.
                                                            (62)

Take no thought for the morrow, for the morrow shall take
thought for the things of itself. Sufficient unto the day is the evil
thereof.   (158)

Use not to-day what to-morrow will need.
Leave to-morrow till to-morrow.
To-morrow's victory shall crown the conflict of to-day.
                                                            (62)

To-day a man—to-morrow a mouse.
When a friend asks, there is no to-morrow.
To-morrow is the reaping of to-day.   (13)
The remedy of to-morrow is too late for the evil of to-day.

On Procrastination.

One of these days is none of these days.
What may be done at any time will be done at no time.
Be discreet, but with discretion urge to quickest action;
Be discreet, but dread delay, the cankerworm of duty.   (62)
They whose work hath no delay achieve Herculean labors.
                                                            (62)

Many undo themselves by delays; they think to do that
hereafter which they never live to do. Practice is the life of all.
                                                            (45)

Night visions may befriend,
Our waking dreams are fatal.   (8)
Thoughts of work without attempting
    Bring moodiness and despair;
For a man may swim in the waters,
    But he cannot swim in air.   (6)

The sooner the better—delay is fetter.
Shun delays, they breed remorse:
    Take thy time while time is lent thee;
Creeping snails have weakest force;
    Fly their fault lest thou repent thee;
Good is best when soonest wrought;
Ling'ring labors come to naught.   (138)
He that surely doth at once the matters to be done
Hath not himself to blame for any ruinous delay.   (62)
Procrastination is the thief of time:
Year after year it steals, till all are fled,
And to the mercies of a moment leaves
The vast concerns of an eternal scene.   (8)
To-day, if ye will hear His voice, harden not your hearts.
(156)

    To-morrow!
It is a period nowhere to be found
In all the hoary registers of Time,
Unless, perchance, in the fool's calendar.   (210)
At thirty, man suspects himself a fool;
Knows it at forty, and reforms his plan;
At fifty chides his infamous delay,
Pushes his prudent purpose to resolve;
In all the magnanimity of thought
Resolves and re-resolves; then dies the same.   (8)
Let us not linger here then, until fate
Make longing unavailing, hope too late,
And turn to lamentations all our prayers.   (207)
    Pray mind this: this is a habit of mind which is very apt
to beset men of intellect and talent, especially when their time
is not regularly filled up, and left to their own arrangement.
(29)

On Early Rising.

The morning hour has gold in its mouth.
In the morning ye shall see the glory of the Lord.   (191)
Rise early and you will observe; labor and you will have.
Ye shall rise up early and go on your way.   (191)

The kingdom of heaven is like unto a man that is a householder who went out early in the morning to hire laborers. (158)

The early riser is healthy, cheerful and industrious.
He who doth not rise early never does a good day's work.
I myself will awake right early. (156)
It is not the early rising, but the well spending of the day.
Up in the morning early,
And leave off being surly.
If you do not rise early you can make progress in nothing. (203)

Early rest makes early rising sure. (7)

Late hours in bed present an index to character, and an omen of the ultimate hopes of the person who indulges in this habit. (206)

Early Rising—a Habit of the Ancients.

Abraham rose up early in the morning.
Abimelech rose up early in the morning.
Jacob rose up early in the morning.
Early in the morning Laban arose.
The Lord said to Moses: Rise up early in the morning and stand before Pharaoh.
Moses rose . . . early in the morning.
Joshua rose up early in the morning.
Gideon rose up early in the morning.
Elkanah and Hannah rose up in the morning early.
David rose up early in the morning.
Job rose up early in the morning.
Darius rose very early in the morning.
I taught them—rising up early and teaching them. (159)

And in the morning, a great while before day, He (Christ) rose up and went out. (199)

On Hurry—Everybody's Remedy for Neglect.

A short cut is often a wrong cut.
What is the best thing to do in a hurry? Answer: Nothing. (197)

59

Always in a hurry, always behind.

He that leaves the highway for a short cut commonly goes about.

A hasty man is seldom out of trouble.

Hasty judgments are generally faulty ones.

Be not hasty in thy spirit to be vexed!   (192)

Most haste, worse speed!

Hastily and well never meet.

Tarry a little that we may make an end the sooner.   (190)

Seest thou a man that is hasty in his words? There is more hope of a fool than of him.   (27)

Anger and haste hinder good counsel.

Haste is slow.

Every one that is hasty hasteth only to want.   (27)

Of hasty counsel take good heed, for haste is very rarely speed.

Nothing in haste but catching fleas.

He that hath an evil eye hasteth after riches.   (27)

Call me not olive, before you see me gathered.

He that hasteth with his feet misseth his way.   (27)

Precipitate counsel—perilous deeds.

Do not hurry, do not flurry!

Nothing good is got by worry.

Haste trips up its own heels.

Hasty climbers have sudden falls.

Hasty resolutions seldom speed well.

I said in my haste: "All men are liars!"   (156)

The Magnitude of Trifles.

A point is the beginning of magnitude.   (200)

Duration, which is endless, could not be but for the moment, which is too finite to be fixed.   (161)

From trivial things great contests oft arise.

Happy and wise is the man to whose thought existeth not a trifle.   (62)

In conduct don't make trifles of trifles.

The mass of trifles makes magnitude.   (123)

Despise not a small wound, a poor kinsman, or a humble enemy.

It is but the littleness of man that seeth no greatness in a trifle. (62)

True delicacy, that most beautiful heart-leaf of humanity, exhibits itself most significantly in little things. (72)

White ants pick a carcass clean sooner than a lion will. (123)

For every shade of difference is a color to keen eyes,
And those who doat on trifles see a mole-hill as a mountain. (62)

Feather by feather the goose is plucked.
A little each day is much in a year.
Your clock within one twelvemonth ticketh thirty million
    seconds,
By steadily without a stop fulfilling small details. (62)

Things to their perfection come,
Not all at once, but some and some.
Hair by hair makes the head bare.
A journey of a thousand miles is begun with a step.
Much of happiness is missed through mere neglect of trifles,
Much of good-doing destroyed for lack of tact and manner. (62)

A pendulum travels much, but it only goes a tick at a time.
Small habits well pursued betimes
May reach the dignity of crimes. (38)

He that is faithful in a very little is faithful in much; and he that is unrighteous in a very little is unrighteous in much. (158)

A mole-hill every minute is a mountain in the year. (62)

He that would make a golden gate must bring a nail to it daily.

Every day a thread makes a skein in the year.
It ever was the gift of genius to build grandeur out of
    trifles.—
Davy's watch-glass, Newton's apple, yielded mighty truths. (62)

Little and often makes a heap in time.
Little strokes fell great oaks.

61

Honesty in little things is not a little thing.

Fire begins with little sparks, crime begins with evil thoughts

The deepest wretchedness of life is continuance of petty pains. (62)

He that contemneth small things shall fall by little and little. (10)

A little fire burns up a great deal of corn. (101)

Step by step one goes far.

Vast is the mighty ocean, but drops have made it vast.
(62)

Little things are great to little men. (3)

Little things please little minds.

Trifles lighter than straws are levers in the building up of character. (62)

Every day is a little life, and our whole life is but a day repeated.

The little ills of life are the hardest to bear. (201)

A mote in the gunner's eye is as bad as a spike in the gun. (62)

It is a great thing to do a little thing well.

Add pence to pence, for wealth comes hence.

Slender joys often repeated, fall as sunshine on the heart.
(62)

The magnitude of most of the trifles that affect us be altered by our way of looking at them. (123)

Well done, good and faithful servant; thou hast been faithful over a few things; I will set thee over many things; enter thou into the joys of thy Lord. (158)

On Endurance, Cheerfulness, Contentment and Patience.

The bird that flutters least is longest on the wing. (7)

Prolonged endurance tames the bold. (184)

Who faints not, achieves.

He bears misery best that hides it most.

Go not for every grief to the physician, for every quarrel to the lawyer, nor for every thirst to the pot. (70)

Behold, we call them blessed which endured. (165)

If ye endure chastening, God dealeth with you as with sons. (41)

Endure hardness, as a good soldier of Jesus Christ. (41)

Thus did Job continually.

Cheerfulness is an excellent wearing quality.

Cheerfulness has been called the bright weather of the heart.

Cheerfulness gives harmony to the soul and is a perpetual song without words.

Content, though mean, and cheerful if not gay. (7)

A rational repast;
Exertion, vigilance, a mind in arms,
A military discipline of thought,
To foil temptation in the doubtful field,
And ever-waking ardor for the right—
'Tis these first give, then guard a cheerful heart. (8)

Piety is cheerful as the day. (7)

One is scarcely sensible of fatigue while he marches to music. (33)

Cheerfulness opens, like spring, all the blossoms of the inward man. (205)

Be cheerful, man of care; for great is the multitude of chances. (62)

Cheerfulness enables nature to recruit its strength.

A cheerful spirit moveth quick—
A grumbler in the mud will stick.
Sweet is the recompense it brings,
The work that with goodwill is done. (63)

Not few nor light are the burdens of life; then load it not with heaviness of spirit. (62)

Cheerfulness is one man's welcome, and the other warneth from him by his gloom. (62)

He who sings, drives away sorrow.

Be always as cheerful as ever you can,
For few will delight in a sorrowful man.

Cheerfulness smoothes the road of life.

There never was contentment in a mean and sordid aim,
And selfish pleasure as an end is always disappointment.
(62)

Doth the wild ass bray when he hath grass? Or loweth the oxen over his fodder? (164)

I have as much as the most, if I have as much as I desire. (211)

Content is a vessel not built for display.
Tho' she's ready and steady, come storm when it may. (109)

Content is the true riches, for without it there is no satisfying. (62)

Be content; the sea hath fish enough.
Contentment walks
The sunny glade, and feels an inward bliss
Spring o'er his mind, beyond the pow'r of kings to purchase. (5)

Contentment wears the hues of joy. (32)

Better bring thy mind to thy condition than have thy condition brought to thy mind.

Generally those who boast most of contentment have least of it. (1)

A lazy hand is no argument of a contented heart. (1)

Hope for the best, get ready for the worst, and then take what God chooses to send. (52)

Contentment is the philosopher's stone, which turns all it toucheth into gold; the poor man is rich with it and the rich man is poor without it.

Try these:
A kind thought—
A kind word—
And a good deed. (257)

A competence is vital to content. (8)

He has enough who is content.

Contentment comes of the heart, not of the house.

Content is health to the sick and riches to the poor.

Contentment consisteth not in heaping more fuel, but in taking away some fire. (1)

Contentment finds *multum in parvo*: it hath a quick eye with which to spy out benefits.

Contentment from a little gift.

A heap of precious joy will sift.
This is the charm, by sages often told
Converting all it touches into gold;
Content can soothe, where'er by fortune placed—
Can rear a garden in the desert waste. (202)

If others' purses be more fat,
Why should we groan and grieve at that?
And great store is great care, the rather if it mightily increaseth;
Albeit too little is a trouble, yet too much shall swell into an evil. (62)

If fortune give thee less than she has done,
Then make less fire, and walk more in the sun. (196)

Our content is our best having. (32)

A harder lesson to learne continence.
In joyous pleasure than in grievous paine. (119)

Ye have need of patience. (41)

Let patience have its perfect work, that ye may be perfect and entire, lacking in nothing. (165)

Patience and resignation are the pillars of human peace on earth. (8)

How poor are they who have no patience!
What wound ever did heal, except by degrees? (32)

You will never repent of being patient and sober.
Patient doth conquer by out-suffering all. (212)

Patience is the ballast of the soul. (213)

Patience adorns the woman, and improves the man; is loved in a child, praised in a young man, admired in an old man; she is beautiful in either sex in every age. (204)

'Tis easy enough to be pleasant,
When life flows by like a song;
But the man worth while,
Is the man with a smile,
When everything goes dead wrong. (264)

Patience in cowards is tame hopeless fear;
But in brave minds, a scorn of what they bear. (37)

The greatest and sublimest power is often simple patience.
(25)

An ounce of patience is worth a pound of brains.

Bring forth fruit with patience. (158)

Patience surpasses learning.

Job was not so miserable in his sufferings, as happy in his patience.

Patient waiting is often the highest way of doing God's way. (24)

Patience is the best buckler against affronts.

The patient in spirit is better than the proud in spirit.
(192)

The daily martyrdom of patience shall not be wanting of reward. (62)

Life's trials may be hard to bear, but patience can outlive them. (62)

Apelles was not a master-painter in one day.

Patience with deserving ever winneth due reward. (62)

The Lord will not fail to come though he may not come on horseback.

To wait and be patient soothes many a pang.

All commend patience, but none can endure to suffer.

If you'd learn patience superfine,
Go you to fish with rod and line.

He that gets patience and the blessing which Preachers conclude with, hath not lost his pains. (4)

Tribulation worketh patience, and patience hope. (41)

If we hope for that we see not, then do we with patience wait for it. (41)

In your patience ye shall win your souls. (158)

The Lord direct your hearts into the love of God, and into the patience of Christ. (41)

Wondrous is the strength of Cheerfulness.

On Punctuality and Habit.

Punctuality is the soul of business.

Punctual as lovers to the moment sworn. (8)

Now, is the watchword of the wise;
Now, is on the banner of the prudent. (62)

One today is better than ten tomorrows.

Now is the constant syllable ticking from the clock of time. (62)

Habit is second nature.

Habit ever remains.

The wisest habit is the habit of care in the formation of habits. (6)

Give the mouse a hole and wonder not that the cheese is taken.

Habits are soon assum'd; but when we strive
To strip them off, 'tis being flayed alive. (7)

All in man is association and habit. (21)

Ill habits gather by unseen degrees,
As brooks make rivers, rivers run to seas.
Inveterate habits choke the unfruitful heart,
Their fibres penetrate its tenderest part.
And, draining its nutritious power to feed
Their noxious growth, starve every better seed. (7)

Man is a bundle of habits. (190)

There is not a quality of function either of body or mind which does not feel the influence of habit. (190)

In the great majority of things, habit is a greater plague than ever afflicted Egypt. (208)

On Criticism.

A false balance is not good. (27)

A perfect judge will read each work of wit
With the same spirit that its author writ. (2)

Criticism, as first introduced by Aristotle, was meant as a standard of judging well. (79)

True ease in writing comes from art, not chance—
As those move easiest who have learned to dance. (2)

Every writing critic is bound to show himself capable of being a writer. (214)

Let such teach others who themselves excel
And censure freely who have written well,
Authors are partial to their wit 'tis true;
But are not critics to their judgment too? (2)

It is not the eye for faults, but beauties, that constitutes the real critic.

Words are like leaves; and where they most abound,
Much fruit of sense beneath is rarely found.   (2)

But true expression, like th' unchanging sun
Clears, and improves whate'er it shines upon.
It gilds all objects, but it alters none.   (2)

Ah ne'er so dire a thirst of glory boast,
Nor in the critic let the man be lost!
Good nature and good sense must ever join;
To err is human, to forgive divine.   (2)

The struck eagle stretched upon the plain,
No more through rolling clouds to soar again,
Viewed his own feather on the fatal dart,
And winged the shaft that quivered in his heart;
Keen were his pangs, but keener far to feel
He nursed the pinion which impelled the steel,
While the same plumage that had warmed his nest,
Drank the last life-drop of his bleeding breast.   (168)

On Bravery, Boldness, Courage, Determination, Persistence, Steadfastness and Tenacity of Purpose.

Walt Whitman was only a hospital nurse serving without pay. He wore no uniform nor badge of office. But when Lincoln saw him, coatless, with bared throat, walking by, he recognized a brother and involuntarily exclaimed, "There goes a Man!"
(257)

A man who will not flee will make his foes flee.
Quit you like men—be strong.   (41)
Foot firm, and faith fast.
Stand still till storm past.
A man of courage never wants a weapon.
Who, with a courage of unshaken root,
In honor's field advancing his firm foot,
Plants it upon the line that justice draws,
And will prevail or perish in her cause;
'Tis to the virtues of such men, man owes
His portion in the good that Heaven bestows.   (7)

A man without courage is a knife without an edge.

Boldness in business is the first, second, and third thing.

The tree does not fall at the first stroke.

Screw your courage to the sticking place, and you will *not* fail.

Resolve to perform what you ought; perform without fail what you resolve. (14)

Always at it wins the day.

Confidence never smiles again upon the man, big or little, who has been beaten at all points. (273)

Thou shalt be steadfast, and shalt not fear. (164)

He who does not tire, tires adversity.

Boldness is akin to power; yea, because ignorance is weakness,
Knowledge with unshrinking might will nerve the vigorous hand. (62)

A brave retreat is a grave exploit.

Courage consists not in hazarding without fear, but in being resolutely minded in a just cause.

A noble fortitude in ills, delights
Heaven, earth, ourselves; 'tis duty, glory, peace.
Affliction is the good man's shining scene;
Prosperity conceals his brightest ray. (8)

We must be made fast to something that is fast, if we are not to be swept like thistledown before the wind. (123)

None sends his arrow to the mark in view,
Whose hand is feeble or his aim untrue. (7)

Be ye steadfast, unmovable, always abounding in the work of the Lord. (41)

Because He is at my right hand, I shall not be moved.
(156)

On Dress.

Finery is foolery.

The woman whose price was above rubies (*see* Proverbs xxxi) *made her own dresses.* (215)

It is a hard matter to dress age and deformity into beauty. (21)

Fond pride of dress is sure a dreadful curse;
It shows an empty head and makes an empty purse.
It is better that a coat should fit the conscience than that
it should fit only the body. (161)

Affectation in dress always misses the end it aims at, and
raises contempt instead of admiration. (21)

A foolish woman is known by her finery.
Husbands that cannot be restrained by duty, will not long
be kept by dress. (21)

Sacrifice to dress, till household joys and comforts cease.
(7)

Negligence in dress is an error that ought to be corrected.
(21)

A fine woman can do without fine clothes.
The power of dress is very great in commanding respect.
(21)

Costly thy habit as thy purse can buy,
But not expressed in fancy; rich, not gaudy;
For the apparel oft proclaims the man. (32)

What a weak hold has that woman of her husband's heart
who ties him only with a curl of ribbon! (21)

I was naked and ye clothed me. (158)

He hath sent me . . . . to give them . . . . the garment of
praise for the spirit of heaviness. (186)

If there come into your synagogue a man with a gold ring,
in fine clothing; and there come in also a poor man in coarse
clothing; and ye have regard to him that weareth the fine clothing, and say, "Sit thou here in this good place," and ye say to
the poor man, "*Stand* thou there," or, "Sit under my footstool;"
do ye not make distinctions? And are ye not become judges
with evil thoughts? (165)

He that created the body hath, by creating it, pledged Himself to provide its raiment. To provide raiment is a smaller act
than creating the body—"the body is *more* than raiment." The
greater includes the less. (161)

Be not anxious . . . . for your body, what ye shall put on. Is
not the . . . . body more than raiment? . . . . Why are ye anxious
concerning raiment? Consider the lilies of the field, how they

grow; they toil not, neither do they spin; yet I say unto you, that even Solomon in all his glory was not arrayed like one of these. But if God so clothe the grass of the field, which to-day is, and to-morrow is cast into the oven, shall He not much more clothe you, O ye of little faith?   (158)

On Pleasure.

Lose no chance of giving pleasure. (64)

Pleasure is due only when all duty's done. (9)

That the soul be without pleasure is not good any more than that it be without knowledge. (6)

Call'd to the Temple of impure delight,
He that abstains—and he alone—does right. (7)

Diseases are the taxes on pleasures.
Pleasure is deaf when told of future pain. (7)

She that liveth in pleasure is dead while she liveth. (41)

He that resisteth pleasures crowneth his life. (10)

Mortals, whose pleasures are their only care,
First wish to be imposed on, and then are. (7)

Girls who cast their ends for pleasure, do not live, but last. (22)

Pleasure is good, and man for pleasure made;
But pleasure full of glory as of joy—
Pleasure, which neither blushes nor expires. (8)

With caution taste the sweet Circean cup;
He that sips often at last drinks it up. (7)

The greatest pleasure of life is love. (115)

When pleasure violates, 'tis then a vice,
And vengeance too—it hastens into pain. (8)

The reward of unlawful pleasure is lawful pain.
Religion does not censure or exclude
Unnumbered pleasures harmlessly pursued. (7)

Early delights cannot long survive. (123)

Reverberated pleasures fire the breast. (8)

Pleasure admitted in undue degree
Enslaves the will, nor leaves the judgment free. (7)

Sure as night follows day,
Death treads in Pleasure's footsteps round the world,
When Pleasure treads the path which Reason shuns.   (8)

If a wish wander that way, call it home:
He cannot long be safe whose wishes roam.   (7)

Tangible pleasures are enough for the animal man.   (62)

Give pleasure's name to naught, but what has passed
Th' authentic seal of reason, and defies
The tooth of time; when passed, a pleasure still.   (8)

On Slander.

Who by aspersions throw a stone
At the head of others, hit their own.   (4)

In a walking newspaper, the leading article is scandal.

He who pelts every barking cur must pick up many stones.

Slander is the homage which vice pays to virtue.

He who repeats the ill he hears of another is the true slanderer.

To stop the tongue of slander stop your own.

Aspersion is the babbler's trade;
To listen is to lend him aid.   (7)

He that blows in the dust fills his own eyes.

Inquire and inquire; for report is a liar.

Slander expires at a good woman's door.

He that uttereth a slander is a fool.   (27)

Believe not every tale.   (10)

Face it out and live it down, whatever be the slander,
And walk on in wise quietness, as utterly unconscious.   (62)

The man that dares traduce, because he can,
With safety to himself, is not a man.   (7)

It is a certain sign of an ill heart to be inclined to defamation.   (107)

If thou hast heard a word let it die with thee.   (10)

A false tale is a nimble footman.

All are not thieves that dogs bark at.

Slander! Slander! some of it always sticks.

To have slanders forgotten by others, forget them yourself.

When men speak ill of thee, live so as nobody may believe them.

He who handles pitch besmears himself.

He who blows upon dust fills his eyes with it.

A false balance is an abomination to the Lord; but a just weight is His delight.

The north wind driveth away rain; so doth an angry countenance a backbiting tongue. (27)

Calumny would soon die and starve if nobody took it in and gave it lodging. (57)

The pure in heart are slow to credit calumnies. (113)

On Appearances.

Be truly what thou wouldst be thought to be.

Their hearts may be fountains whose eyes are flints, and may inwardly bleed who do not outwardly weep. (1)

There is a way which seemeth right unto a man; but the end thereof are the ways of death. (27)

Thus 'tis with all; their chief and constant care
Is to seem everything but what they are. (3)

To affect always to be the best of the company argues a base disposition. (1)

Don't rely on the label on the bag.

Every scratch in the hand is not a stab to the heart; nor doth every false opinion make a heretic. (1)

The heart that means well will never wish to seem ill, for commonly we affect to show better than we are.

How easy is pen and paper piety for one to write religiously? I will not say it costeth nothing, but it is far cheaper to work one's head than one's heart to goodness. (1)

If any man among you seem to be religious and bridleth not his tongue, but deceiveth his own heart, this man's religion is vain. (165)

On Home.

There the good angel of the house, the mother, wife and
    mistress,
With gentle care and thoughtful love is ministering life.
(62)

East or west, home is best.

The place to spend a happy day—Home.

There the cheerful daughters plan their charities for all,

There with no eye service, but in honest faith and truth,

The family domestics work, and worship with their betters.

(62)

Men make houses, but women make homes.

No man can safely go abroad who does not love to stay at home. (18)

There's no place like home.

The curse on the hearth wounds the deepest.

For every heart the thought of home will bring its special difference,

As varying truth may testify to sorrows or to joys. (62)

He is the happiest, be he king or peasant, who finds peace in his home. (36)

Enmity, extravagance, contempt, wrath, strife, envy, opposition—

These be the seven devils possessing the unholy hearth.

(62)

Water, smoke and a vicious woman, drive men out of the house.

On Promising.

All promise is poor dilatory man; and that through every stage. (8)

A promise delayed is justice deferred.

A promise attended to is a debt settled.

A promise neglected is an untruth told.

Things promised are things due.

A promise is a debt that we may not forget.

A promise should be given with caution and kept with care.

A promise and its performance should, like the scales of a true balance, always present a mutual adjustment.

Promises make debts and debts promises.

A promise against law or duty is void in its own nature.

A false promise thou must shun,

'Tis a lie and theft in one.

A promise should be made by the heart and remembered by the hand.

A promise is the offspring of the intention, and should be nurtured by recollection.

When thou dost purpose aught within thy power,
Be sure to do it, though it be but small;
Constancie knits the bones, and makes us stowre,
When wanton pleasures beckon us to thrall.
Who breaks his own bond, forfeiteth himself;
What nature made a ship he makes a shelf.   (4)

On Temper.

Bad temper bites at both ends. It makes one's self nearly as miserable as it does other people.

If you lose your temper don't look for it.

Good temper oils the wheels of life.

How spite cankers things.   (4)

Temper is a revelation of an unloving nature at bottom.   (65)

He submits to be seen through a microscope who suffers himself to be caught in a passion.   (59)

The peculiarity of ill temper is that it is the vice of the virtuous.   (65)

Temper is so good a thing that we should never lose it.

A stone is heavy, and the sand weighty; but a fool's vexation is heavier than them both.   (27)

Cease from anger, and forsake wrath; fret not thyself, it tendeth only to evil-doing.   (156)

Vexation killeth the foolish man.   (164)

He that is hasty of spirit, exalteth folly.   (27)

On Providence.

You know not where a blessing may light.

For a web begun God sends thread.

As a wise man, if wiser, would deal with himself, so the Divine Providence deals with him.   (6)

Even in small things there is great providence.

If God bolts the door do not get through the window.

Thou mayest take small heed, thou hast counted it a chance; but that which now hath flowered, groweth on old roots. (62)

Heaven deigns to suit our trials to our strength. (38)

The protection which we have is protection in, and not protection from strife and danger. (123)

When ae door steeks anither opens.

Every thread and every ray is a miracle of care; a miracle of mercy too, unless thy folly scorn it; a miracle of wisdom, whatever be thy thought. (62)

The eyes of all wait upon Thee, and Thou givest them their meat in due season. Thou openest Thine hand, and satisfiest the desire of every living thing. (156)

On Wisdom.

A man was killed by a circular saw, and in his obituary it was stated that he was "a good citizen, an upright man, and an ardent patriot, but of limited information regarding circular saws."

Wisdom is rare.

Thou think'st it folly to be wise too soon! (8)

Days should speak and multitude of years should teach wisdom. (164)

Despise not the discourse of the wise, but acquaint thyself with their proverbs. (10)

Incline thine ear unto wisdom. (27)

The man of wisdom is the man of years. (8)

Wisdom is the wealth of the wise.

If thou seest a man of understanding, get thee betimes unto him, and let thy foot wear the steps of his door. (10)

How much better is it to get wisdom than gold! (27)

Wisdom is a good purchase though we pay dear for it.
The Lord *giveth* wisdom. (27)

What is not wisdom is danger.

Buy wisdom, and instruction, and understanding. (27)

Pay down the cost—whatever it be: and the cost will be something of *self*. (161)

Reason stands small show against the entrenched power of habit. (257)

Say unto wisdom: Thou art my sister. (27)

Wisdom less shudders at a fool than wit. (8)

A man shall be commended according to his wisdom. (27)

Wisdom is neither inheritance nor legacy.
The mouth of the just bringeth forth wisdom. (27)

Wisdom is not harsh-voiced and frowning, but benignant and approachable. (6)

The wisdom of the prudent is to understand his way. (27)

He that getteth wisdom loveth his own soul. (27)

Wise it is to comprehend the whole. (8)

Wisdom *resteth* in the heart of him that hath understanding. (27)

A hero or a genius or both, is the man who guesses right most of the time and then does it.

I have seen wicked men and fools, a great many of both, and I believe they get paid in the end; but the fools first. (260)

Wealth may seek us; but wisdom must be sought,
Sought before all; but (how unlike all else
We seek on earth!) 'tis never sought in vain. (8)

Thou art wise, if thou beat off petty troubles, nor suffer their stinging to fret thee. (62)

Cease from thine own wisdom. (27)

'Tis greatly wise to talk with our past hours,
And ask them what report they bore to heaven,
And how they might have borne more welcome news;
Their answers form what men experience call. (8)

Whoso loveth wisdom rejoiceth his father. (27)

Wisdom is a loving spirit. (11)

Her conversation hath no bitterness. (11)

Wisdom is a defence. (192)

Where one is wise two are happy.
Where two discourse, if the one's anger rise,
The man who lets the contest fall is wise. (94)

Get wisdom, get understanding; forget it not. (27)

Wisdom is profitable to direct. (192)

A counsellor of good things and a comfort in cares and grief. (11)

A man's wisdom maketh his face to shine (to look cheerful). (192)

Wisdom is ofttimes nearer when we stop than when we soar. (85)

Whoso watcheth for her (wisdom) shall quickly be without care. (11)

Wisdom is better than rubies; and all the things that may be desired are not to be compared unto her. (27)

No mention shall be made of coral, or of pearls; for the price of wisdom is above rubies. (164)

Wisdom is too high for a fool. (27)

You may be an ardent worker,
　　But, no matter what you do,
Always watch the other fellow,
　　For he may be working you.
Don't take any undue chances,
　　Always to yourself be true;
Work your neighbor on the quiet
　　While he's planning to work you.
Think all you speak, but speak not all you think.
　　Thoughts are your own; your words are so no more.
Where Wisdom steers, wind cannot make you sink.
　　Lips never err when Wisdom keeps the door. (219)

She shall lead me soberly in my doings and preserve me in her power. (11)

In much wisdom is much pain. (192)

My heart was troubled in seeking her; therefore have I gotten a good possession. (10)

With the lowly is wisdom. (27)

Be not wise in thine own eyes! (27)

A wise man doesn't need advice, and a fool won't take it. (257)

They whom truth and wisdom lead
Can gather honey from a weed. (7)

Wisdom without goodness is craft and treachery. (21)

Wisdom is glorious and never fadeth away; yea, she is easily seen of them that love her, and found of such as seek her. She preventeth them that desire her, in making herself first known unto them. Whoso seeketh her early shall have no great travail; for he shall find her sitting at his doors. (11)

Wisdom is good with an inheritance. (192)

Wisdom is better than weapons of war. (192)

We deem those men remarkable who think as we do. (257)

Wisdom prefers an unjust peace to a just war.

The rod and reproof give wisdom. (27)

The multitude of the wise is the welfare of the world. (11)

There is no wisdom, nor understanding, nor counsel *against* the Lord. (27)

All wisdom is on the side of the Lord. (161)

Knowledge is proud that he has learned so much; Wisdom is humble that he knows no more. (7)

Wise men in the world are like timber trees in a hedge, here and there one.

Tools die for want of wisdom. (27)

He is wise that hath wit enough for his own affairs.

He that is void of wisdom despiseth his neighbor. (27)

To be allied unto wisdom is immortality. (11)

Superior wisdom is superior bliss. (8)

When a man reaches the age of about forty years, he then spends much of his time taking inventory of those things which he thought he knew, and sifting out that which is of no account.

With the well-advised is wisdom. (27)

I perceived that I could not otherwise obtain her, except God gave her me. (11)

Wisdom is better than strength. (192)

If things were to be done twice, all would be wise.

The well-spring of wisdom is as a flowing brook. (27)

No one so wise but has a little folly to spare.

Into a malicious soul wisdom shall not enter; nor dwell in the body that is subject unto sin. (11)

Great men are not always wise. (164)

Wisdom is the principal thing; therefore get wisdom; and with all thy getting, get understanding. Exalt her, and she shall promote thee; she shall bring thee to honour, when thou dost embrace her. She shall give to thine head an ornament of grace; a crown of glory shall she deliver to thee. (27)

It is more easy to be wise for others than for thyself. (27)

If thou be wise, thou shalt be wise for thyself. (27)

Wisdom is not vicarious. (161)

When either side grows warm with argument, the wisest man gives over first.

A wise son maketh a glad father. (27)

Let not the wise man glory in his wisdom! (159)

Go to the ant . . . . consider her ways, and be wise! (27)

The sublimity of wisdom is to do those things living, which are to be desired when dying. (80)

When wisdom entereth into thine heart, and knowledge is pleasant unto thy soul; discretion shall preserve thee, understanding shall keep thee. (27)

Wise men care not for what they cannot have.

Wise-mindedness in each should govern lust, and ire, and —its own self. (162)

He that walketh with wise men shall be wise. (27)

The lips of the wise shall preserve them. (27)

Be wisely worldly, but not worldly wise. (50)

A wise servant shall have rule over a son that causeth shame. (27)

Better is a poor and wise child than an old and foolish king. (192)

He that begetteth a wise child shall have joy of him. (27)

The wise shall understand. (218)

Whoso keepeth the law is a wise son. (27)

I would have you wise unto that which is good. (41)

Happy is the man that *findeth* wisdom, and the man that getteth understanding. For the merchandise of it is better than the merchandise of silver, and the gain thereof than fine gold. She is more precious than rubies; and all the things thou canst desire are not to be compared unto her. Length of days is in her right hand; and in her left hand riches and honour. Her ways are way of pleasantness, and all her paths are peace. She is a tree of life to them that lay hold upon her; and happy is every one that retaineth her. (27)

The mouth of the righteous speaketh wisdom. (156)

They that be wise shall shine as the brightness of the firmament; and they that turn many to righteousness as the stars for ever and ever. (218)

Be ye wise as serpents, and harmless as doves. (158)

If any of you lack wisdom, let him ask of God—who giveth to all men liberally, and upbraideth not—and it shall be given him. (165)

Thoughts on Being True and Pure.

Truth seeks no corners.

Righteousness is a straight line, and is always the shortest distance between two points. (161)

Cleanliness is a fine life-preserver.

Buy the truth and sell it not. (27)

If thou art in company with others, be not ashamed of Truth. (62)

Craft must have clothes, but truth loves to go naked.

I know of no more encouraging fact than the unquestionable ability of a man to elevate his life by a conscious endeavor. It is something to be able to paint a particular picture or to carve a statute, and so make a few objects beautiful; but it is far more glorious to carve and paint the very atmosphere and medium through which we look, which morally we can do. (275)

Whatsoever things are true, whatsoever things are honest, whatsoever things are just, whatsoever things are pure . . . . think on these things. (41)

God loves good accounts.

Dress and undress thy soul; mark the decay and growth of it. (4)

Chastity is either abstinence or continence. (21)

This nation never stood in greater need than now of having among its leaders men of lofty ideals, which they try to live up to and not merely to talk of. We need men with these ideals in public life, and we need them just as much in business and in such a profession as law. (262)

The very rich man who conducts his business as if he believed that he were a law unto himself, thereby immensely increases the difficulty of the task of upholding order when the disorder is a menace to men of property; for if the community feels that rich men disregard the law where it affects themselves, then the community is apt to assume the dangerous and unwholesome attitude of condoning crimes of violence committed against the interests which in the popular mind these rich men represent. (262)

It is far more important that they should conduct their business affairs decently than that they should spend the surplus of their fortunes in philanthropy. (262)

Every man of great wealth who runs his business with cynical contempt for those prohibitions of the law which by hired cunning he can escape or evade, is a menace to our community; and the community is not to be excused if it does not develop a spirit which actively frowns on and discountenances him. (262)

We all know that as things actually are many of the most influential and highly remunerated members of the bar in every center of wealth make it their special task to work out bold and ingenious schemes by which their very wealthy clients, individual or corporate, can evade the laws which are made to regulate, in the interest of the public, the use of great wealth.
(262)

The great lawyer who employs his talent and his learning in the highly remunerative task of enabling a very wealthy client to override or circumvent the law is doing all that in him lies to encourage the growth in the country of a spirit of dumb anger against all laws and of disbelief in their efficacy. (262)

The sure-enough saint is a business man who sticks to the one-price system and tells the truth. (257)

A chaste eye exiles licentious looks.

He that pleads against the truth takes pains to be overthrown. (50)

What obvious truth the wisest heads may miss! (7)

Simple truth was ever wisdom, even among liars. (62)

A truth-teller finds the doors closed against him.

There is no error so crooked, but it hath in it some lines of truth. (62)

As for the pure his work is right. (27)

Truth finds foes where it makes none.

There is nothing so false, that a sparkle of truth is not in it. (62)

He that loveth pureness of heart, for the grace of his lips the king shall be his friend. (27)

Unto the pure all things are pure. (41)

Truth is the best buckler.

The words of the pure are pleasant words. (27)

Spurn not at seeming error, but dig below its surface for the truth;

And beware of seeming truths, that grow on the roots of error. (62)

There is nothing so true that the damps of error have not warped it. (62)

Love rejoiceth in the truth. (41)

There is no widespread error that hath not truth for its beginning. (62)

Even from the body's purity, the mind receives a secret sympathetic aid. (5)

His heart cannot be pure whose tongue is not clean.

Whatever purifies fortifies also the heart. (96)

Who lives well sees afar off. (99)

Void of purity in morals, faith is but a hypocrite of words. (62)

The righteous shall hold on his way, and he that hath clean hands shall wax stronger and stronger. (164)

On Disciplinary Trouble (Care, Pain, Grief, etc.); Undeserved Trouble, and Trouble Which is Self-Inflicted or Imaginary.

What smarts, teaches.
Each day has its care, but each care has its day.
Pain past is pleasure.
Sorrow is surgery. (6)

Neither our own power nor the world's help can we know without trial. (6)

If you have the "blues," read the twenty-seventh Psalm. If your pocket-book is empty, read the thirty-seventh Psalm. If people seem unkind, read the fifteenth chapter of John. If you are discouraged about your work, read the one hundred twenty-sixth Psalm. If you are all out of sorts, read the twelfth chapter of Hebrews. If you can't have your own way in everything, keep silent and read the third chapter of James. If you are losing confidence in men, read the thirteenth chapter of First Corinthians.

It is our own fault if we are overwhelmed by the tasks, or difficulties, or sorrows of life. (123)

A juggler's instant skill hath been long years alearning. (62)

Things hardly attained are longer retained.

Sorrows remembered sweeten present joy. (9)

Know how sublime a thing it is to suffer and be strong. (12)

Sorrow which is never spoken is the heaviest load to bear. (64)

Grief divided is made lighter.

A pensive soul feeds upon nothing but bitters.

Nothing is so foolish or wretched as to anticipate misfortunes. (30)

Misfortunes when they come are ever found more light to bear than expectation dreaded. (62)

If misfortune comes, she brings along the bravest virtues. (5)

Heaviness in the heart of a man maketh it stoop; but a good word maketh it glad.

Great griefs are mute.

'Tis impious in a good man to be sad. (8)

Every substantial grief has twenty shadows, and most of them shadows of your own making.

A hundred years of fretting will not pay a single cent of debt.

Much pain must expite what much pain procur'd. (8)

Pain is useful unto man, for it teacheth him to guard his life. (62)

It is worse to apprehend than to suffer. (92)

Fretting cares make gray hairs.

Light cares speak, great ones are dumb. (30)

Be careful or you may be full of cares. (56)

We know that the whole creation groaneth and travaileth in pain together (with us) until now. (41)

Affliction cometh not forth of the dust, neither doth trouble spring out of the ground; but man is born unto trouble, as the sparks fly upward. (164)

The righteous is delivered out of trouble. (27)

By sorrow of heart the spirit is broken. (27)

Roll thy burden upon the Lord and He shall sustain thee. (156)

My son, regard not lightly the chastening of the Lord, nor faint when thou art reproved of Him; for whom the Lord loveth He chasteneth, and scourgeth every son whom He receiveth. (27)

God shall wipe away every tear from their eyes; and death shall be more; neither shall there be mourning, nor crying nor pain any more: the first things (the dispensation of discipline) have passed away. (157)

Surely He hath borne our griefs, and carried our sorrows. (186)

When He giveth quietness, who can make trouble? (164)

Ye shall be sorrowful, but your sorrow shall be turned into joy. (158)

On That Which is Good.

For the average mind precedent sanctifies. (257)

Good things go in a small compass.

A good thing is soon snatched up.

A good recorder sets all in order.

It is good for a man that he bear the yoke (be under discipline) in his youth. (159)

Good company in a journey is worth a coach.

A good head will get itself hats.

A good horse never lacks a saddle.

A good thing, if you know it—do it.

A good horse cannot be of a bad color.

The good man standeth calm and strong, for God is his ally. (62)

Good words cost no more than bad.

Good words and no deeds are rushes and reeds.

Good words cost nothing and are worth much.

Good words cool more than cold water.

Good take heed doth surely speed.

Good ware make a quick market.

It is good fishing in troubled waters.

A good man shall be satisfied from himself. (27)

A good name is a sound inheritance.

A good action is never thrown away.

Good comes out of evil.

Good watch prevents misfortune.

The good we never miss we rarely prize. (7)

A good goose may have an ill gosling.

A good man shall obtain favor of the Lord. (27)

A good layer-up should be a good layer out.

Goodness is the supreme beauty. (155)

A good understanding have all they that keep the commandments of God. (156)

Be good, and let heaven answer for the rest. (8)

There is no good that doth not cost a price. (63)

There is a difference between profanity and dramatic fervor. (257)

A good man leaveth an inheritance to his children's children. (27)

A good name keeps its luster in the dark.

Good understanding giveth favor. (27)

A good thing is all the sweeter when won with pains.

Good tidings make the bones fat. (27)

A good worker should have good wages.

A good name is rather to be chosen than great riches; and loving favor rather than silver and gold. (27)

A good word maketh the heart glad. (27)

Keep good humor still, whate'er we lose. (2)

A word in due season—how good is it!   (27)

It is good for me that I have been chastened; that I might learn thy statutes.   (156)

It is good to be zealously sought in a good matter at all times.   (41)

It is a good thing—to give thanks unto the Lord;—to sing praise unto Thy name, O most high;—to show forth Thy loving-kindness in the morning;—and Thy faithfulness every night.
(156)

It is good that a man should hope and quietly wait for the salvation of the Lord.   (159)

The steps of a good man are ordered by the Lord.   (156)

Love sought is good, but given unsought is better.   (32)

On That Which is Better.

Good management is better than good income.
Not to break is better than to mend.
Better ne'er hae begun nor ne'er end it.
Better to have than to wish.
A bad custom is like a good cake, better broken than kept.
Health is better than wealth.
Better, therefore, ride alone, than have a thief's company.
(1)

A cripple in the right is better than a racer in the wrong.
Better short of pence than short of sense.
The poorest truth is better than the richest lie.
Of two evils choose the least.
Of two evils choose neither (if you can help it)
Better late than never.
Better never late.
The law of love is better than the love of law.
Better be than seem.
Better say nothing than nothing to the purpose.
Better be poor than wicked.
A good name is better than a girdle of gold.
Better that the feet slip than the tongue.
Better go back than go wrong.
Better to show too much civility than too little.
Ae bird i' the hand is worth ten fleeing.   (69)

Better break your word, than do worse in keeping it.

A lean compromise is better than a fat lawsuit.

Better late thrive than never do well.   (69)

Better to be done than wish it had been done.

It is better to dwell in the corner of the housetop, than with a contentious woman in a wide house.

Better be silent than speak ill.

Better is a dinner of herbs where love is, than a stalled ox and hatred therewith.   (27)

A civil denial is better than a rude grant.

Wisdom is better than strength . . . and better than weapons of war.   (192)

A friend's frown is better than a fool's smile.

Better is the end (completion) of a thing than the beginning thereof; and the patient in spirit is better than the proud in spirit.   (192)

Better is a poor and wise youth than an old and foolish king.   (192)

Better be troubled *for* sin than *by* sin.

A good hope is better than a bad possession.

Give me the ass that carries me, in preference to the horse that throws me.

A servant that dealeth wisely shall have rule over a son that doeth shamefully.   (27)

A good fame is better than a good face.

Better is it thou shouldest not vow (resolve), than that thou shouldest vow and not pay (perform).   (192)

Better keep peace than make peace.

Better is open rebuke than love that is hidden.   (27)

Creditors have better memories than debtors.

Advise not what is most pleasant, but what is most useful.   (220)

It is better to dwell in a desert land, than with a contentious and fretful woman.   (27)

An injury forgiven is better than an injury revenged.

Better is a poor man than a liar.   (27)

How much better is it to get wisdom than gold!   (27)

Better is a little with righteousness, than great revenues with injustice.   (27)

Better the error of love than the love of error.

A good name is better than precious ointment; and the day of death than the day of one's birth. (192)

Better than the mighty is he that is slow to anger; and he that ruleth his spirit than he that taketh a city. (27)

Better is a dry morsel and quietness therewith, than a house full of feasting with strife. (27)

It is better to go to the house of mourning, than to go to the house of feasting: for that is the end (perfecting) of all men and the living will lay it to his heart. (192)

Two are better than one; because they have a good reward for their labor. For if either fall the one will lift the other up. (192)

Better is a little with the fear of the Lord, than great treasure and trouble therewith. (27)

It is better to hear the rebuke of the wise than for a man to hear the song of fools. (192)

Better is it to be of a lowly spirit with the poor, than to divide the spoil with the proud. (27)

Sorrow is better than laughter: for by the sadness of the countenance the heart is made glad. (192)

Better is the poor that walketh in his integrity than he that is perverse in his lips and is a fool. (27)

Better is he that is lightly esteemed, and hath a servant, than he that honoreth himself and lacketh bread. (27)

The life of love is better than the love of life.

It is the deliberate verdict of the Lord Jesus that it is better not to live than not to love. (65)

Live thy better, let thy worst thoughts die. (83)

On That Which is Best and the Best that Can be Done Under the Circumstances.

The best things are not bought and sold. (63)

Whate'er is best administer'd is best. (7)

The best sauce is hunger.

The best ground bears weeds as well as flowers.

The best colt needs breaking in.

The best merchants never best each other.

The best eyes look inward and upward.

The best laid schemes of mice and men gang aft a-gley.
(28)

The best cast at dice is not to play.

The best of men are but men at the best.

The best cause requires a good pleader.

The best fish swim near the bottom.

The best cloth may be devoured by moth.

Best to bend it while it is a twig.

The best is the cheapest in the end.

If you pay nothing, don't grumble about the score.

If you can't help, don't hinder.

Leave it if you cannot mend it.

There is nothing so well done but may be mended.

Don't blame it, but better it.

I will not meddle with that I cannot mend. (1)

On Authors and Books.

He who proposes to be an author should first be a student.
(33)

There is no worse robber than a bad book. (70)

A good book is the best companion.

It is a man's duty to have books . . . A library is not a luxury, but one of the necessaries of life. (230)

Every book that we take up without a purpose is an opportunity lost of taking up a book with a purpose. (237)

God be thanked for books! (224)

Books are the Glasse of Counsell to dress ourselves by.
(223)

Books support us in solitude, and keep us from being a burden to ourselves. (225)

Wondrous, indeed, is the virtue of a true book. (33)

In the highest civilization the book is still the highest delight. (226)

What is a great love of books? It is something like a personal introduction to the great and good men of all past times. (228)

Books are the windows through which the soul looks out. (230)

A great book that comes from a great thinker . . . is a ship of thought, deep-freighted with truth and beauty. (227)

Precious and priceless are the blessings which books scatter around our daily paths. (231)

Of bad books we can never read too little; of the good, never too much. (235)

He who has published an injurious book sins, as it were, in his grave; corrupts others, while he is rotting himself. (236)

A good book is the precious life-blood of a master spirit. (26)

Except a living man, there is nothing more wonderful than a book! (232)

Whosoever acknowledges himself to be a zealous follower of truth . . . must of necessity make himself a Lover of Books. (222)

Would you know whether the tendency of a book is good or evil examine in what state of mind you lay it down. (234)

Avoid especially that class of literature which has a knowing tone: it is the most poisonous of all. Every good book, or piece of book, is full of admiration and awe. It may contain firm assertion or stern satire, but it never sneers coldly nor asserts haughtily; and it always leads you to reverence or love something with your whole heart. (44)

A common book will often give you much amusement, but it is only a noble book which will give you dear friends. (44)

If when I read a book about God, I find it has put Him farther from me; or about man, that it has put me farther from him . . . *that,* for me, is a bad book . . . I shall come nearer to my fellows, and God nearer to me, or the thing is a poison. (233)

Books are the masters who instruct us without rods and ferrules, without hard words and anger, without clothes or money. (222)

I would prefer to have one comfortable room well stocked with books to all you could give me in the way of decoration which the highest art can supply. (228)

No book is worth anything which is not worth *much.* (44)

To know the true value of books, and to derive any satisfactory benefit from them, you must first feel the sweet delight of buying them—you must know the preciousness of possession. (239)

We ought to reverence books, to look at them as useful and mighty things. If they are good and true . . . they are the message of Christ, the Maker of all things—the Teacher of all truth. (232)

Always read the preface to a book. It . . . enables you to survey more completely the book itself. You frequently also discover the character of the author from the preface. (238)

On Sense and Wit.

No sense so uncommon as common sense.
Plain sense but rarely leads us far astray. (8)
There are forty men of wit to one of sense.
A deluge of words and a drop of sense.
A handful of common sense is worth a bushel of learning. (99)

Use your wit as a buckler, not as a sword.
Our senses, as our reason, are divine. (8)
Wit ill applied is a dangerous weapon.
Wit talks most, when least she has to say, and reason interrupts not her career. (8)
Worldly wise is but half-witted, at its highest praise. (8)

On Tact and Discretion.

If you have a loitering servant, place his dinner before him, and send him on an errand. (99)
Policy goes beyond strength.
Little wit in the head makes much work for the feet.
Fair and softly goes far.
Discreet women have neither eyes nor ears. (102)
Not every word requires an answer.
Contrivance is better than force.
Cleverness is as dexterity of the fingers—only of worth when under the control of kindness and wisdom. (6)

Don't keep your coals in a volcano.   (241)

Horses will do more for a whistle than for a whip.   (1)

On Gossip.

Don't advertise: tell it to a gossip!

Thou shalt not go up and down as a tale-bearer among thy people.   (191)

A gossip and a liar are as like as two peas.

A gossip in a village is like a viper in a bed.

Where there is no tale-bearer contention ceaseth.   (27)

A gossip and a liar, like as bramble and briar.

The words of a whisperer are as dainty morsels.   (27)

Gossips and tale-bearers set on fire all the houses they enter.

He that listens for what people say of him shall never have peace.

A tale-bearer revealeth secrets.   (27)

A gossip is the lucifer match of the village.

None are so fond of secrets as those who don't mean to keep them.

On Gambling—the Sport of all Sports.

Gambling is an express train to ruin.

Horse-racing is a galloping consumption.

Ducks lay eggs: geese lay wagers.

Gambling is play in name, but crime in reality.

Wealth gotten by vanity shall be diminished.   (27)

He who gambles picks his own pocket.

The devil goes shares in gaming.

A wager is a fool's argument.

The man who takes a wager when he has won it is simply thieving by consent of the loser—he has no right to anything of his neighbor's without giving value for it—a present only excepted.   (161)

Gambling is but one remove from theft, and both are the offspring of covetousness.   (161)

The best throw of the dice is to throw them away.

He that bets is a better, and he that does not bet is no better. (242)

On Obstinacy and Rashness.

What is the use of running when we are not on the right road?

Do not in an instant what an age cannot recompense. (1)

The robes of lawyers are lined with the obstinacy of clients.

Two Sir Positives can scarce meet without a skirmish.

An obstinate heart shall be laden with sorrows. (10)

Love is the only fire that is hot enough to melt the iron obstinacy of a creature's will. (123)

To scare a bird is not the way to catch it.

If you cannot heal the wound do not tear it.

Who perisheth in needless danger is the devil's martyr.

Do no such things which, done once, are done for ever, so that no bemoaning can amend them. (1)

In thy rage make no Persian decree which cannot be reversed or repealed; but rather Polonian laws, which (they say) last but three days. (1)

He that would heal a wound must not handle it.

Seeing that these things cannot be gainsaid, ye ought to be quiet and do nothing rash. (240)

On Order and Method.

Order is heaven's first law. (26)

All is soon ready in an orderly house.

Let all things be done decently and in order. (41)

Order is the sanctity of the mind, the health of the body, the peace of the city, the security of the state.

To choose time is to save time; and an unseasonable motion is but beating the air. (19)

One day is as good as two for him who does everything in its place.

Let all your things have their place; let each part of your business have its time. (14)

On Oath-taking.

An unlawful oath is better broke than kept.

An oath is not needed by a good man, nor will it prevent the bad man from perjuring himself.   (161)

An oath demands "the truth, the whole truth, and nothing but the truth." Why should there be less when the oath is not administered?   (161)

I say unto you: Swear not at all; neither by heaven, for it is God's throne; nor by the earth, for it is His footstool . . . Neither shalt thou swear by thy head, because thou canst not make one hair white or black. But let your communication be: Yea; Nay. Whatsoever is more than these (any extra assertion) cometh of evil.   (158)

On Self in Its Many Moods and Tenses.

He that doth what he will oft doth what he ought not.

He who won't be advised, can't be helped.

Rule lust, temper and tongue, and bridle the belly.

He that can reply calmly to an angry man is too hard for him.

He has wit at will that wi' an angry heart can haud him still.

Leave unsaid the wrong thing at the tempting moment.

If everyone would mend one, all would be amended.

Self-love nobody else's love.

A bridle for the tongue is a necessary piece of furniture.

For what thou canst do thyself rely not on another.

To be the hero of selfish imaginings is the subtle poison of pride.   (62)

We cloak our sins from ourselves with many wrappings.   (123)

No man is the worse for knowing the worst of himself.

No man can safely speak who does not willingly hold his tongue.   (18)

Self-love is a mote in every man's eye.

A man may have a just esteem of himself without being proud.

He overcomes a stout enemy that overcomes his own anger.

The selfish heart deserves the pain it feels. (8)

Fling from thy clean hand the viper of self-righteousness. (62)

Everyone should sweep before his own door.

He who knows himself best esteems himself least.

It is not our changing circumstances, but our unregulated desires that rob us of peace. (123)

Whoever takes it for his law to do as he likes will not for long like what he does. (123)

It is no breach of contentment for men, by lawful means, to seek the removal of their misery and bettering of their estate. (1)

He will never get to heaven that desires to go thither alone.

Passion may be hot and strong, but thou canst be its master, unless thy silly weakness yield the battle to thy foe. (62)

Thoughts—Words—Deeds.

Invective and vituperation are all right, in their places, but men who have nothing else to offer do not stay long in the game. Only the doers and thinkers last. (257)

The school of Christ is much harder to get a diploma from than from Princeton, Yale, or any other college. (265)

A right thought is as a true key. (6)

A thinking man is always striking out something new.

Thought, too, deliver'd is the more possess'd. (8)

If you think twice before you speak once, you will speak twice the better for it.

Man is known by his thoughts and devisings, and so is the Maker of men. (6)

Expression is the dress of thought.

Speech, thought's canal! speech, thought's criterion too. (8)

A long tongue is a sign of a short hand.

Fit words are fine; but often fine words are not fit.

Evil words cut worse than swords.

Words once spoken cannot be wiped out with a sponge.

Self-reliance is the name we give to the egotism of the man who succeeds. (257)

A word once out flies everywhere.

A man that breaks his word bids others be false to him.

Refrain not to speak when there is occasion to do good. (10)

A word and a stone let go cannot be recalled.

A wise man will hold his tongue till he see opportunity. (10)

He who is scared by words has no heart for deeds.

Works—not words—are the proof of love.

A man's good intentions seldom add to his income.

Words show the wit of man, but actions his meaning.

Talk like Robin Hood when you can shoot with his bow.

On Depreciating, Grumbling and Censuring.

The man who is always having his feelings hurt is about as pleasing a companion as a pebble in a shoe. (257)

Any little silly soul easily can pick a hole.

Faint praise is often strong censure.

False weights and measures short eschew
And give to every man his due.

Care for no man's censure, unless conscience countersign it. (62)

He who findeth fault meaneth to buy

Faint praise is akin to abuse.

Murmuring unfits the soul for duty.

Shallow wits censure everything that is beyond their depth.

When the maid leaves the larder door open the cat's in fault.

Blame not before thou hast examined the truth. (10)

Grumbling makes the loaf no larger.

He must be pure who would blame another.

The absent always bear the blame.

Beware of murmuring, which is unprofitable. (11)

Growling will not make the kettle boil.

The absent are always at fault. (102)

There are some of us who seem to think that we compliment God's heaven by despising His earth, and show our sense of the great things the future man may do yonder, by counting as utterly worthless all that the present man may do here. (6)

On Gluttony, Greediness, Moderation and Abstinence.

Ninety-nine people out of a hundred who go to a physician have no organic disease, but are merely suffering from some symptom of their own indiscretion. (257)

Look to thy mouth; diseases enter there. (4)

You dig your grave with your teeth.

Let thine appetite survive its temperate repast. (62)

Abstain from all appearance of evil. (41)

A dainty stomach beggars the purse.

Grasp not at much, for fear thou losest all. (4)

Milk the cow, but don't pull off the udder.

Covetousness brings nothing home.

Covetousness disbelieveth God, and laugheth at the rights of men. (62)

For covetousness never had enough, but moaneth at its wants forever. (62)

Greediness bursts the bag.

The drunkard and the glutton shall come to poverty. (27)

Covetousness often starves other vices.

Covetousness is the hunger which comes from eating.

Covetousness is the punishment of the rich.

Gluttony is evil—and starvation. (62)

Add to your knowledge temperance. (166)

Moderation is the silken string running through the pearl-chain of all virtues. (1)

Let your moderation be known among all men. (41)

Let pleasure be ever so innocent, the excess is always criminal. (107)

All excess is bad—abstinence, as intemperance. (62)

Moderation is not a halting betwixt two opinions, when the thorough believing of one of them is necessary to salvation. (1)

On Example, Consistency, Genuineness, Faithfulness, Honesty and Influence.

Were every one to sweep before his own house, every street would be clean.

Precepts may lead—but examples draw.

We live in an age that hath more need of good examples than precepts. (4)

The parent's life is the child's copy-book. (13)

As the old birds sing, the young ones twitter.

Will not a man listen? Be silent; and prove thy maxim by example;

Never fear, thou losest not thy hold, though thy mouth doth not render a reason. (62)

Conduct has the loudest tongue. (7)

A good example is the best sermon.

An indulgent mother makes a sluttish daughter.

Be sparing of advice by words, but teach thy lesson by example. (62)

Christ suffered for you, leaving you an example, that ye should follow His steps. (166)

People look at my six days in the week, to see what I mean on the seventh. (40)

I have given you an example, that you should do as I have done to you. (158)

When the dam leaps over, the kid follows.

Who goes himself is in earnest; who sends is indifferent.

True sincerity sends for no witness.

A conscientious liar is one who has misrepresented a matter so long that even he himself believes it to be as he says. (257)

Who don't keep faith with God won't keep it with man.

The will steadfast to the truth—this is fidelity.

The heart assured by the truth—this is confidence. (6)

A good gaper makes two gapers.

He who persists in genuineness will increase in adequacy. (6)

When you obey your superior, you instruct your inferior.

Make the night night, and the day day, and you will live happily. (99)

It becomes not a law-maker to be a law-breaker. (104)

Be the same thing that ye wad be ca'd. (69)

A wise man scorneth nothing, be it never so small or homely. (62)

The consciousness that some are hearing, cometh as a care;
The sense that some are watching near, bindeth thee to caution. (62)

The rotten apple injures his neighbor.

The people who influence you are people who believe in you. (65)

A sentence hath formed a character, and a character subdued a kingdom. (62)

Stars teach as well as shine. (8)

An honest man is not the worse because a dog barks at him.

A picture hath ruined souls, or raised them to commerce with the skies. (62)

Many love to praise right and do wrong.

It is a good thing, and a wholesome, to search out bosom sins. (62)

A specious show of honesty cometh as the herald of a thief. (62)

An honest man's the noblest work of God. (28)

Mind hath its influence on mind; and no man is free but when alone. (62)

Of all crafts, to be an honest man is the master-craft.

Honesty is exact to a penny.

The hypocrite of honesty; ye may know him by an over-acted part;
Taking pains to turn and twist, where other men walk straight. (62)

On Fear, Expectation, Anticipation and Hope.

Fear kills more than the physician.

Fear will make thee wretched, though evil follow not behind. (62)

He who would gather roses must not fear thorns.

A man too careful of danger liveth in continual torment. (62)

Foolish fear doubleth danger.

Fear no ill but sin, no being but Almighty God. (9)

Go up to your fears and speak to them, and they will generally fade away. (123)

Expectation is the fool's income.

The sting of pain, and the edge of pleasure are blunted by long expectation;

For the gall and balm alike are diluted in the waters of patience. (62)

Her worth shines forth the brightest, who in hope confides. (112)

Hope, that paints the future fair. (29)

Hope deferred maketh the heart sick, but when the desire cometh, it is a tree of life. (27)

He may hope for the best that's prepared for the worst.

He that wants hope is the poorest man alive.

If winter come, can spring be far behind. (77)

Hope is the only tie which keeps the heart from breaking. (1)

Hope is grief's best music.

He has no hope that never had a fear. (7)

We are saved by hope. (41)

On Calmness, Restfulness and Forbearance.

Man's greatest strength is shown in standing still. (8)

The way to make thy sonne rich is to fill his minde with rest, before his trunk with riches. (4)

Correct thy son, and he shall give thee rest. (27)

If the soul be full of tumult and jangling noises, God's voice is little likely to be heard. (123)

Come unto Me, all ye that are weary and heavy laden, and I will give you rest. Take My yoke upon you, and learn of Me; for I am meek and lowly in heart: and ye shall find rest unto your souls. (158)

Rest in the Lord, and wait patiently for Him. (156)

The tooth often bites the tongue, and yet they keep together.

A little explained, a little endured, a little passed over as a foible,

And lo, the jagged atoms fit like smooth mosaic. (62)

Husband, don't see! wife, be blind!

To rude words turn deaf ears.

Thou canst not shape another's mind to suit thine own body,
Think not, then, to be furnishing his brain with thy special
notions. (62)

A wise man in a crowded street winneth his way with gentleness, nor rudely pusheth aside the stranger that standeth in his path. (62)

If we would mirror God, our souls must be calm. (123)

Whiles a man liveth he may mend; count not thy brother reprobate. (62)

Fret not thyself, it tendeth only to evil doing. (156)

Mildness governs more than anger. (241)

A look, or a word, or an act, may be taken well or ill,
As construed by the latitude of love, or the closeness of
cold suspicion. (62)

A disputable point is no man's ground. (7)

Tolerant wisdom is content to suffer all phases of opinion,
For shrewd experience of men seeth infinite variety in character. (62)

On Experience and Worth.

Experience keeps a dear school, but fools will learn in no other. (14)

A thing lost is a thing known,
Every man's experience is a lesson due to all. (62)

What you learn to your cost you remember long.

Damage suffered makes you knowing, but seldom rich.

We may give advice, but we cannot give conduct. (14)

What costs nothing is worth nothing.

Each man is a man, and may have his individuality of work and worth. (6)

On Temptation—Sought, Shunned, Endured.

He who keeps off the ice will not slip through.
No one can be caught in places he does not visit.
If you don't touch the rope you won't ring the bell.
Harming is warning.

102

If the camel once gets his nose into the tent, his whole body will enter.

If you walk on a tight rope, you'll need a balancing pole.

Harm watch—harm catch.

Temptation once yielded to gains power. (123)

He who avoids the temptation avoids the sin. (99)

Every man is tempted when he is drawn away of his own lusts and enticed. (35)

They that desire to be rich fall into a temptation and a snare, and many foolish and hurtful lusts, such as drown men in destruction and perdition. (41)

There hath no temptation taken you but such as is common to man. (41)

Blessed is the man that endureth temptation, for when he is tried he shall receive the crown of life. (165)

On Giving and Taking Offense: Bearing and Inflicting Injuries: Revenge, Disputing, Argument, Wrangling, Quarreling and The Passions.

Neither give nor take offense.

They hurt themselves that wrong others.

Nothing is ill said if it is not ill taken.

He that acknowledges not his sin, he maketh a double offense. (10)

Avoid extremes; forbear resenting injuries. (14)

The offender never pardons.

He invites future injuries who rewards past ones.

The remedy for injuries is not to remember them.

Chiefly be thou ware of this, an unforgiving spirit. (62)

Wrong none by doing injuries, or omitting the benefits that are your duty. (14)

The noblest remedy of injuries is oblivion.

Revenge commonly hurts both the offerer and sufferer.
(20)

The best sort of revenge is not to be like him who did the injury. (97)

To forget a wrong is the best revenge.

It costs more to revenge injuries than to bear them.

In taking revenge, a man is but even with his enemy; but in passing it over, he is superior.

He is above his enemies that despises their injuries.

If slighted, slight the slight, and love the slighter.

Answer not before thou hast heard the cause: neither interrupt men in the midst of their talk. (10)

Take away fuel, take away flame.

Wranglers are never in the wrong.

Contradiction should awaken attention, not passion.

As coals are to burning coals, and wood to fire; so is a contentious man to kindle strife.

In too much disputing truth is lost.

Great disputing repels truth.

Opposition gives opinion strength. (7)

Beware of entrance into a quarrel. (75)

No foolery to falling out.

Two cannot fall out if one does not choose.

A quarrelsome man never lacks words.

A good man will as soon run into fire as a quarrel.

When two quarrel both are in the wrong.

The second blow makes the fray.

When one will not, two cannot quarrel. (99)

Old quarrels and old charges are best left alone. Raise no unsavory odors. If evil will die, let it die.

It takes two to make a quarrel.

Be not the first to quarrel, nor the last to make it up.

Every fool will be quarreling. (27)

On Fortitude, Firmness and Thoroughness.

Half heart is no heart.

There be companies and seasons where resolute bearing is but duty. (62)

Fortitude is victory. (3)

Valor that parlays is near yielding.

Many fearless chiefs have won the friendship of a foe. (62)

Many would be cowards if they had courage enough.

104

The iron will of one stout heart shall make a thousand quail. (62)

Calamity is the touchstone of a brave mind.

Confidence is conqueror of men; victorious both over them and in them. (62)

The surest way not to fail is to determine to succeed. (88)

A resolute purpose knitteth the knees, and the firm tread nourisheth decision. (62)

Without danger, danger cannot be surmounted. (241)

He that hunts two hares will catch neither.

Plough deep and you will have plenty of corn.

A little of everything is nothing in the main.

Half-doing is many a man's undoing.

A timid man has little chance.

If you wish a thing done, go; if not, send.

I hate to see a thing done by halves; if it be right, do it boldly; if it be wrong, leave it undone. (130)

A stroke at every tree, without felling any.

The wise and prudent conquer difficulties by daring to attempt them. (74)

Intentions which die are pretensions which lie.

On Fame, Notoriety, Ambition, Aspiration; Giving and Receiving Praise; Merit, Reputation and Character.

Tall trees catch much wind.

He that pitches too high won't get through his song.

Fondness for fame is avarice of air. (8)

Ambition, the last infirmity of noble minds. (26)

Fame is the perfume of heroic deeds. (167)

Peace begins just where ambition ends. (8)

Widely as we stretch our reverent conceptions, there is ever something beyond. (123)

Everybody says it, nobody knows it.

Common fame is much to blame.

No ruins are so irreparable as those of reputation. (21)

It shall be small care to the high and happy conscience, what jealous friends, or envious foes, or common fools may judge.
(62)

If you would be in good repute, let not the sun find you in bed.

True nobility is invulnerable.

A good reputation is a fair estate.

A good name is to be chosen rather than great riches.   (27)

Purity of motive and nobility of mind shall rarely condescend to prove its rights, and prate of wrongs, or evidence its worth to others.   (62)

Men of character are the conscience of the society to which they belong.   (55)

A little mind courteth notoriety, to illustrate its puny self.   (62)

Let another man praise thee, and not thine own mouth.
(27)

Never raise your own praise.

Praise is rebuke to the man whose conscience alloweth it not.   (62)

Never man was praised, but that praise provoked a censure.
(62)

Never man was censured, some one standeth forth to praise.
(62)

It is a sign of a good man, if he grows better for commendation.

On their own merits modest men are dumb.

If a liar accuseth thee of evil, be not swift to answer:

Yea, rather give him license for awhile; it shall help thine honor afterwards.   (62)

To well deserve is somewhat, in spite of ill success.   (62)

On Necessity, Poverty, Need and Dependence.

Necessity sharpens industry.

Man wants but little, nor that little long.   (8)

Thou say'st, 'tis needful: Is it therefore right?   (8)

The crowd is faced because they must, and not because they like it.   (62)

Necessity is a hard nurse, but she raises strong children.

A fine cage won't feed the bird.

He bears poverty very ill who is ashamed of it.

That's but an empty purse which is full of other men's money.

Saints must come to poverty, if prudence be not theirs. (62)

It is astonishing how little one feels poverty when one loves. (121)

Power hath ordained nothing which Economy saw not needful. (62)

Your Heavenly Father knoweth what things ye have need of before you ask Him. (158)

My God shall fulfil every need of yours according to His riches in glory in Jesus Christ. (41)

On Forethought, Reflection, Deliberation and Choice.

Our nature such, ill choice ensures ill fate. (8)

You must judge a maiden at the kneading trough, and not in a dance.

Pluck the rose and leave the thorns.

Deliberating is not delaying.

Be slow in choosing, but slower in changing.

Measure thrice before you cut once.

Fore-think, though you cannot fore-tell.

Take a vine of good soil, and a daughter of a good mother.

Let reason go before every enterprise, and counsel before every action. (10)

A little oil may save a deal of friction.

We wisely strip the steed we mean to buy. (8)

One false move may lose the game.

What's none of my profit shall be none of my peril.

If thou wilt apply thy mind thou shalt be prudent. (10)

Prudence looketh unto faith, content to wait solutions. (62)

Caution is the parent of safety.

A little fore-talk may save much after-talk.

Be slow enough to be sure.

Too much caution, too much rashness, both alike are harmful. (62)

On Ingratitude, Impurity, Sensuality, Impatience, Indecision, Insincerity, Ignorance, Injustice, Unkindness, Weakness, Wickedness.

Never cast dirt into that fountain of which thou hast sometime drank. (101)

Be not ungrateful to your old friend.

The man was never yet found who would acknowledge himself guilty of ingratitude. (32)

Amongst men, it is as ill taken to turn back favors as to disobey commands. (1)

Meddle with dirt and some of it will stick to you.

The man is dead who for the body lives. (8)

A long crepe veil often hides a tickled to death countenance. (261)

A false balance is abomination to the Lord; but a just weight is His delight.

Ingratitude doth not only stop the flowing of more mercy, but even spills what was formerly received. (1)

From eye, and ear, and tongue, and touch, and thought, reject all lewdness. (62)

Ignorance is the mother of impudence.

That pilgrim is base that speaks ill of his staff. (99)

A too quick return of an obligation is a sort of ingratitude.

A dirty tale should neither be told nor heard.

Uncleanness is the parent of blindness of mind. (21)

The heart does not think all the mouth says.

Ignorance shuts its eyes and swears that it sees.

Wonder is the daughter of ignorance.

Where ignorance is bliss 'tis folly to be wise.

While thou thinkest of many things thou thinkest of nothing; while thou wouldst go many ways thou standest still.

Of ten lepers, only one returned to give thanks, which shows that by nature, without grace over-swaying us, it is ten to one if we be thankful. (1)

No cut like unkindness.

Not to know some trifles is a praise. (2)

He that worketh wickedness by another is wicked himself.

A man who has not learned to say, "No!" will be a weak and a wretched man till he dies—and after.

Wickedness, condemned by her own witness, is very timorous, and being pressed with conscience, always forecasteth grievous things. (11)

Fright not people from thy presence with the terror of thy intolerable impatience. (1)

Ye'll brak' your neck as soon as your fast i' his house. (69)

A man of an ill tongue is dangerous in his city. (10)

He who knows nothing is confident of everything.

Ignorance is less hateful than conceitedness.

On Life, Death, Disease, the Grave and Resurrection.

Learn as if you were to live for ever; live as if you were to die to-morrow.

The one theme of Ecclesiastes is moderation. Buddha wrote that the greatest word in any language was equanimity. William Morris said the finest blessing of life was systematic, useful work. St. Paul declared the greatest thing in the world was love. Moderation, Equanimity, Work and Love—let these be your physicians, and you will need no other. (257)

A good life keeps off wrinkles.

You have lived if you have loved. (90)

The truest end of life is to know the life that never ends. (95)

Life is enjoyed the most when courted least; most worth when disesteemed. (8)

For honorable age is not that which standeth in length of time, nor that is measured by number of years. But wisdom is the gray hair unto men, and an unspotted life is old age. (11)

Thy life is no idle dream, but a solemn reality.

It is thy own; it is all thou hast to front eternity with. (33)

Narrow is the way which leadeth to life, and few there be that find it. (158)

As gold is given for earnest of gold, so is life given for earnest of life. (6)

Human life is constant want, and ought to be a constant prayer. (84)

Dost thou love life? then do not squander time, for that is the stuff life is made of. (14)

He lives longest that is awake most hours.
That life is long that answers life's great end. (8)

He most lives who thinks most, feels the noblest, acts the best. (49)

A blaze betokens brevity of life. (8)

Individuals who have diseases, nine times out of ten, are suffering from the accumulated evil effects of medication. (257)

The aids to noble life are all within. (73)

The dead make the living dearer. (6)

Most diseases are the result of medication which has been prescribed to relieve and remove a beneficent warning symptom on the part of Nature. (257)

God does not lose us in the dust of death. (123)

Death hath nothing terrible in it but what life hath made.
Think how the fact of dying will solve many a riddle! how much more we shall know by shifting our position! (123)

Death has no advantage but when it comes as a stranger.
(50)

Nature is always and forever trying hard to keep people well, and most so-called "disease"—which word means merely the lack of ease—is self-limiting, and tends to cure itself. If you have no appetite, do not eat. If you have appetite, do not eat too much. Be moderate in the use of everything, except fresh air and sunshine. (257)

Here real and apparent are the same—You see the man. (8)

If death be terrible, the fault is not in death, but thee.
Virtue alone has majesty in death. (8)

Death mows the fairest lilies, as well as the foulest thistles.
Death cuts the saints down, but it cannot keep them down.
The people you see waiting in the lobbies of doctors' offices are, in a vast majority of cases, suffering through poisoning caused by an excess of food. Coupled with this go the bad results of imperfect breathing, improper use of stimulants, lack of exercise, irregular sleep, or holding the thought of fear, jealousy and hate. All of these things, or any of them, will, in very many persons, cause fever, chills, congestion, cold feet and faulty elimination. (257)

There are no greater difficulties in connection with the resurrection, than with the present life. (161)

Disease invades the chastest temperance. (8)

I am the resurrection and the Life; he that believeth on Me though he were dead, yet shall he live; and he that liveth and believeth on Me shall never die. (158)

On Heaven and Hell.

An age more curious than devout is more fond to fix the place of heaven, or hell, than studious this to shun, or that secure. (8)

A hammer of gold will not open the gate of heaven.

Heaven—our soul's own country evermore. (162)

Rejoice that your names are written in heaven. (158)

Those who are bound for heaven must be willing to swim against the stream. (52)

Ye also have a Master in heaven. (41)

The tongue . . . . is set on fire by hell. (165)

Heaven must be in thee, ere thou canst be in heaven.

He will never go to heaven who is content to go alone.

However forgotten, heaven is still thy home. (162)

In my Father's house are many mansions; if it were not so I would have told you: I go to prepare a place for you; and . . . I will come again and receive you unto myself. (158)

Hell is truth seen too late.

Hell is wherever heaven is not.

Hell and destruction are never satisfied. (27)

If I make my bed in hell, behold Thou art there. (156)

Hell is full of the ungrateful.

There are no fans in hell.

Hell is full of good meanings and wishes.

By nature sin is dark, and loves the dark, still hiding from itself in gloom, and in the darkest hell is still itself the darkest hell, and the severest woe, where all is woe. (9)

Whosoever shall say, "Thou fool!" shall be in danger of the hell of fire. (158)

The wicked shall be turned into hell, and all the nations that forget God. (156)

Some Facts and Fair Questions Respecting the Devil.

Your adversary, the devil, as a roaring lion, walketh about, seeking whom he may devour. (166)

Satan will never show himself but to his own advantage.

(1)

The devil can cite Scripture to suit his purpose.

The devil is old, but not infirm.

He who deals with the devil will make small profits.

Satan fashioneth himself into an angel of light. (41)

The devil is good when he is pleased.

If you let the devil into the cart, you'll have to drive him home.

When the devil finds the door shut he retires!

Resist the devil, and he will flee from you. (165)

The God of peace shall bruise Satan under your feet shortly.

(41)

On Wrongdoing, Unbelief, Atheism, Guilt, Repentance, Confession and Absolution.

Most men of the present time have accepted the general content of ethics, but they are slapping at the validity of the principles of Christ. Every one tries to get in a position where he can say in answer to an order to do something: 'I don't have to.'

(265)

A man never gets what he hoped for by doing wrong, or if he seems to do so, he gets something more that spoils it all.

(123)

Error alone needs artificial support, truth can stand by itself. (31)

Error is a hardy plant; it flourishes in every soil. (62)

Harrow hell and rake up the devil.

The rudder of man's best hope cannot always steer himself from error. (62)

None are evil wholly, or evil all at once. (63)

It is human to err, but diabolical to persevere.

To study every great movement we must study the men of the times. The men of the present day seem to be trying to see how near they can come to the prison gates without getting behind them. (205)

He that believeth not God hath made Him a liar. (157)

Might is right and every one tries to get his fellow on the hip. I hate to see a cold-blooded, right living rascal who has $4,000,000 teach a Sunday school class and drive the hardest bargain within the range of the law on week days. (265)

Who is a liar but he that hath denied that Jesus is the Christ? (157)

If we say that we have not sinned, we make God a liar. (157)

By night an atheist half believes a God. (8)

Confess that you were wrong yesterday; it will show that you are wise to-day.

Frailties get pardon by submissiveness. (4)

If you want easier traveling, mend your ways.

Man's most hideous guilt hath grown of zeal for God. (62)

This is to be wretched indeed, to be guilty without repentance.

Man falls by man, if finally he falls. (8)

A fault confessed is half redressed.

A generous confession disarms slander.

Look in fear upon the guilt that might have been thine own. (62)

Men, absolved by mercy from the consequence, forget the evil deed, and God imputes it not. (9)

If we confess our sins, He is faithful and just to forgive us our sins, and to cleanse us from all unrighteousness. (157)

On Sowing and Reaping.

As you make your bed so you must lie on it.
Cent. per cent. do we pay for every vicious pleasure.
If you sow thorns, you will not reap roses.
As you build, such your house.
He that sows iniquity shall reap sorrow.
As you think of others, others will think of you.
Who speaks, sows; who listens, reaps.

With what judgment ye judge, ye shall be judged.

Who undertakes too much, succeeds but little.

The comforter's head never aches. (70)

Loaves put awry into the oven come out crooked.

Who spits against heaven it falls in his face. (99)

An ill life, an ill end.

The measure of charity thou dealest shall be poured into thine own bosom. (62)

What comes from the heart goes to the heart.

If I had not lifted up the stone, you had not found the jewel. (101)

They have sown the wind, and shall reap the whirlwind. (244)

Be not deceived; God is not mocked; for whatsoever a man soweth, that shall he also reap. For he that soweth unto his own flesh shall of the flesh reap corruption; but he that soweth unto the Spirit shall of the Spirit reap eternal life. (41)

Uniformity Impossible.

Let every bird sing its own note.

It is hard to get two heads under one hat.

All bread is not baked in one oven.

All feet cannot wear one shoe.

On Reproof and Correction.

It is a bad coat that will not bear brushing.

Contempt is the sharpest reproof.

He that will not use the rod on his child, his child shall be used as a rod on him. (1)

Correction should not respect what is past, so much as what is to come.

He is well onward in the way of wisdom, who can bear a reproof and mend by it.

The truth of nature, which, with well temper'd satire smoothly keen

Steals thro' the soul, and without pain corrects. (5)

114

It is an ill wool that will not take dye.

Reproofs of instruction are the way of life. (27)

On Knowledge, Learning, Mental Power, Education and Capacity.

If thou wilt, thou shalt be taught. (10)

Many a teacher, lacking judgment, hindereth his own lessons. (62)

We are all very proud of our reason, and yet we guess at fully one-half we know.

If thou love to hear, thou shalt receive understanding. (10)

A little mind is boastful and incredulous, for he fancieth all knowledge is his own. (62)

Thinking is very far from knowing.

Mindfully, with high conscience, true scholars study all things, and learn betimes to use aright all weapons in all armories. (62)

The many-sided mind is ripe for every prize. (62)

Conscience or affection gives strange keenness to the mind. (62)

There is nothing so much worth as a mind well instructed. (10)

Learning is a sceptre to some, a bauble to others.

By falling we learn to go safely.

Reading maketh a full man, conference a ready man, and writing an exact man. (19)

He that is not wise will not be taught. (10)

If we wish to teach, we must stoop to think the scholar's thoughts. (123)

A good education is the best dowry.

The master (teacher) who has forgotten his boyhood will have poor success. (123)

A man knows no more to any purpose than he practises.

Knowledge is not found, unsought, in heaven. (9)

In all regions of life exercise strengthens capacity.

No man hath guessed his capabilities, nor how he shall expand. (62)

The receiver's capacity determines the amount received, and the receiver's desire determines his capacity. (123)

Never yet was mind exhausted, nor one heart dug out. (62)

On Solitude, Asceticism and Isolation.

'Tis converse qualifies for solitude. (8)

The ascetic sinneth as the epicure. (62)

Where there is some truth with but little love, there will be haughty isolation. (6)

To separate ourselves from our brethren is to lose power. (123)

Bless'd retirement, friend to life's decline. (3)

There they live their truest life, and all things show sincere. (62)

No man can safely isolate himself, either intellectually or in practical matters. (123)

They are never alone that are accompanied with noble thoughts. (127)

There never was such a lonely soul on this earth as Christ's because there never was another as pure and loving. (123)

On the Power of the Eye—For Good or Evil.

To the jaundiced all things seem yellow.
The mistress's eye keeps kitchens clean.
If thine eye be evil, thy whole body shall be full of darkness. (158)

It is sure to be dark if you shut your eyes.
The eye of the master makes the horse fat, and that of the mistress the chambers neat.
A common mind perceiveth not beyond his eyes and ears. (62)

Some servants, out of slothfulness, will not run except some do look upon them, spurred on with their master's eye. (1)

One single glance will conquer all descriptions. (62)

If thine eye be single, thy whole body shall be full of light. (158)

116

On Outside Show, Conceit and Humility, (True and False).

"What a dust I have raised," quoth the fly upon the coach.

It is not a sign of humility to declaim against pride.

Some people will never learn anything, because they understand everything too soon.

Don't make your wheat so long in the straw.

If their master takes no account of them, servants will make small account of him, and care not what they spend who are never brought to an audit. (1)

He's not the best carpenter that makes the most chips.

His clothes are worth thousands, but his wit is dear at a penny.

He who commences many things finishes but few.

It needs more skill than I can tell to play the second fiddle well.

He that humbles himself shall be exalted.

The boughs that bear most hang lowest.

On Kindness, Generosity, Gratitude, Justice and Integrity.

All kindness begins in *purpose*.

Fellow-feeling makes us wondrous kind. (245)

A kind face is a beautiful face.

A gift with a kind countenance is a double present.

No enmity so hard and fierce, that kindness cannot melt. (62)

Kind looks foretell a kind a heart within. (9)

Kindness comes o' will.

Kindness will creep whar it mauna gang. (69)

A forced kindness deserves no thanks.

Kind words don't wear out the tongue.

He that walks uprightly walks surely.

To cultivate kindness is a valuable part of the business of life.

Be not forgetful to entertain strangers, for thereby some have entertained angels unawares. (35)

I see there is no such way to have a large heart as to *have* a large heart. (1)

No party his benevolence confin'd—No sect. (5)

An open hand shall have something in it.

Give at first asking what you safely can; 'tis certain gain to help an honest man.

A willing helper does not wait until he is asked.

You may light another's candle at your own without loss.

The seasons come and go, and go and come, to teach men gratitude. (9)

What is justice? To give every man his due. (247)

Keep justice, keep generosity, yielding to neither singly. (62)

On Faith and Creed.

He does not believe that does not live according to his belief.

If weak thy faith, why choose the harder side? (8)

A great mind is ready to believe, for he hungereth to feed on facts. (62)

Who sows his corn in the field trusts in God.

In the worst is ample hope, if only thou hast charity and faith. (62)

Faith is the substance of things hoped for—the evidence of things unseen. (35)

Were there no promised land—no future inheritance—there would be no faith. (161)

Nothing comely, nothing famous, but its praise is faith. (62)

Faith builds a bridge across the gulf of death. (8)

Never was a marvel done upon the earth, but it had sprung of faith. (62)

In faith Columbus found a path across untried waters. (62)

This is a victory which overcometh the world—even our faith. (41)

Christ speaketh to the dead: as those that are capable of living. (62)

Bear with evil, and expect good.

God pleadeth with the deaf, as having ears to hear. (62)

Forms and liturgies and articles may screen truth or display her. (62)

Let bigots fight for creeds, the good man hath the right one. (62)

Garments of every shape are each held the livery for heaven. (62)

Live truly, and thy life shall be a great and noble creed. (67)

On Well-doing and Doing as Well as Possible.

It is not easy to be good nowadays. I would rather write a perfect system of ethics than practise an everyday one. (265)

To do well is to do choicely. (6)

The conscience of well-doing is an ample reward. (30)

Learn the luxury of doing good. (3)

When thy hand hath done a good act, ask thy heart whether it was well done. (1)

Do good by stealth, and blush to find it fame. (2)

Do good and care not to whom.

He who fasteth and doeth no good, saveth his bread, but loseth his soul.

Whoever has heartily done well, has done more than he knew of: God had meaning and purpose in him. He was a weapon as well as a warrior. (6)

If a thing be easy, do it as well as if it were hard.

He does much who does a little well.

Doing good is the only certain happy act of a man's life. (127)

The good you do is not lost, though you forget it.

On Occupation, Diligence and Duty.

Employment is Nature's physician. (87)

Constant occupation prevents temptation. (70)

If simple conscience rest content, thy livelihood is lawful—
Trivial though it seem, allied to ridicule and folly. (62)

Men who can be relied upon are always in demand. The scarcest thing in the world is a thoroughly reliable man. (270)

If thou hast gathered nothing in thy youth, how canst thou find anything in thine age?

Do what you ought, come what may.

A diligence in all things is the strongest fulcrum of success. (62)

He who has well considered his duty will at once carry his conviction into action. (47)

Consult duty, not events. (76)

Duty only frowns when you flee from it; follow it, and it smiles upon you.

The consciousness of duty performed gives us music at midnight. (4)

Duty is a power which rises with us in the morning, and goes to rest with us in the evening. (48)

It fares best with them that are most careful about duty and least about safety. (46)

Duties are ours; events are God's. (40)

He that does what he can does what he ought.

On Jesting.

Take a joke as a joke, and it will not provoke.

Jesting is not unlawful if it trespasseth not in quantity, quality, or reason. (1)

A joke never gains an enemy, but often loses a friend.

A jest driven home too far brings home hate.

He that would jest must take a jest, else to let it alone were best.

It is no joke to bear with a man who is all jokes.

On Opportunity, Neglect, Circumstances, and Being Ready.

Unused advantages are no advantages.

You do not need anything else than negligence to ensure that things will come to grief. (123)

A little neglect may breed great mischief.

There can be no greater slight and dishonor to a giver than to have his gifts neglected. (123)

Where is a sharper arrow than the sting of unmerited neglect? (62)

For a dead opportunity there is no resurrection,
To him that wills ways are not wanting.

He is a good time-server that finds out the fittest opportunity of every action. (1)

Omit no opportunity of doing good, and you will find no opportunity for doing ill.

Success doesn't come to those who wait—and it doesn't wait for anyone to come to it.

Sail while the breeze blows, wind and tide wait for no man.

The day I did not sweep the house there came to it one I did not expect.

Have not the cloak to make when it begins to rain.

OPPORTUNITY.

Master of human destinies am I!
 Fame, love, and fortune on my footsteps wait.
 Cities and fields I walk; I penetrate
Deserts and seas remote, and passing by
 Hovel and mart and palace, soon or late
 I knock unbidden once at every gate.
If sleeping, wake; if feasting, rise before
 I turn away. It is the hour of fate,
 And they who follow me reach every state
 Mortals desire, and conquer every foe
 Save death; but those who doubt or hesitate,
 Condemned to failure, penury, and woe,
Seek me in vain and uselessly implore;
I answer not, and I return no more. (268)

On Secrets.

To him that you tell your secret, you resign your liberty.
The only way to keep a secret is to say nothing.
How will it look by daylight?

What is done by night appears by day.

There is nothing hid that shall not be manifested.   (158)

On Counsel and Advice.

Advice is easier than helping.

Good advice is beyond all price.

Nothing is so liberally given as advice.

Advice when most needed is least heeded.

Take counsel before it goes ill, lest it go worse.

If the counsel be good, no matter who gave it.

There is nothing of which men are more liberal than their good advice.   (8)

Be slow of giving advice, ready to do a service.   (70)

Write down the advice of him who loves you, though you like it not at present.

Good counsels observed are chains to grace.   (1)

On Losses.

He who loses money, loses much; he who loses a friend, loses more; but he who loses his spirits, loses all.   (99)

It is a bad well into which one must put water.

There are losses which are gains, and gains which are losses.

Fortune lost, nothing lost; courage lost, much lost; honor lost, more lost; soul lost, all lost.

What shall it profit a man, if he gain the whole world and lose his own soul?   (158)

He that will save his life shall lose it, and he that will lose his life for My sake shall find it.   (158)

On Virtue and Vice.

Virtue, not rolling suns, the mind matures.   (8)

Virtue consists in action.

Enforced monogamy is society's plan for perpetuating the commonplace.   (257)

Who follow not virtue in youth cannot fly sin in old age.
(70)

Vice is contagious. (21)

The proudest vice is ashamed to wear its own face long.

On Companionship and its Influence.

A crowd is not company.
Associate with men of good judgment.
The presence of a second spirit must control thine own.
(62)

A good companion makes good company. (99)
Bad company is the devil's net.
A wicked man will rob thee of precious time, if he doth no more mischief. (1)

On Morality, Religion, Christianity, Prayer, Worship and God.

The grand morality is love of God. (8)
The religious are not necessarily the good. (6)
Christianity does not so much give us new affections or faculties, as a new direction to those we already have. (38)
Christ is not valued at all unless He be valued above all. (39)

The excess of difficulty is on the side of atheism, not of inspiration. (249)

On Religion—How Can I be Lost?

Just live on without accepting Christ as your Saviour, and you will *never* be *saved.*

The Way to be Saved.

Believe on the Lord Jesus and thou shalt be saved—Acts 16:31.

Forsake thy way—return unto the Lord and He will abundantly pardon—Isa. 55:7.

What profit to *you* if you get money—pleasure, position or power—and in a few short years (at longest) you lose your soul? Matt. 16:26.

Is This a Fact?

There is no other way under heaven to be saved (Acts 4:12)—than by the—"Precious blood of Jesus."—1 Peter 1:18-19.
BIBLE SAYS SO.

To believe on Jesus is simply to take Him at His word.

SO EASY.—*Whosoever* believeth on Me shall have eternal life.—John 3:15, 16.

. . . *There is not the slightest doubt* but that Jesus will forgive your sins and help you if you WILL ASK—for He said: "WHOSOEVER cometh unto Me I will in no wise cast out."—John 6:37.

Can I be Saved at Once?

The jailer believed and was saved SAME NIGHT.—Acts 16:31-34.

The thief believed and was saved SAME DAY.—Luke 23:42-43.

The woman believed and was saved SAME HOUR.—Luke 7:36-48.

Boast not thyself of to-morrow, for thou knowest not what a day may bring forth. Prov. 27:1.

I, YOU will believe YOU can be saved NOW—for Jesus said: "He that believeth HATH (not will have) everlasting life."—John 5:24.

What doth the Lord require of thee, but to do justly, and to love mercy, and to walk humbly with thy God? Micah 6:8.
Insure With the King's Insurance Co.

Capital—Eph. 3:8. "The unsearchable riches of Christ."

Assets—Ps. 24:1, "The earth is the Lord's and the fulness thereof."

Liabilities—2 Cor. 12:9—"My grace is sufficient for thee."

Incontestability—Rom. 8:38, 39, "For I am persuaded that neither death, nor life, nor angels, nor principalities, nor powers, nor things present, nor things to come, nor height, nor depth, nor any other creature, shall be able to separate us from the love of God which is in Christ Jesus our Lord."

Non-forfeitability—Jno. 5:24. "He that heareth my words, and believeth on him that sent me, hath everlasting life, and

124

shall not come into condemnation; but is passed from death unto life."

Eligibility—Rev. 22:17, "WHOSOEVER WILL, let him take the water of life freely."

Conditions—Luke 13:3, "Except ye REPENT, ye shall all likewise perish." Acts 16:31, "BELIEVE on the Lord Jesus Christ, and thou shalt be saved."

Premium—Isa. 55:1, "Without money and without price."

Dividends—Ps. 84:11, "No good thing will he withhold from them that walk uprightly."

Policy—Payable now. Jno. 3:36, "He that believeth on the Son HATH (not will have) everlasting life."

Home Office—Heaven.

Branch Offices—All of God's churches.

Agents—Any true minister of the gospel.

Examiner—The Great Physician—Jesus Christ.

FRIEND, DON'T YOU WANT A POLICY?

NOW IS THE ACCEPTED TIME.

Religion is, in its essence, the most gentlemanly thing in the world. (23)

The elect are the "whosoever-wills," and the non-elect are "whosoever-won'ts." (16)

A Christian is the highest style of man. (8)

I have a great need of Christ; but I have a great Christ for my need.

Godliness is stronger than all. (11)

Pray devoutly and hammer stoutly.

Prayer will make us leave off sinning, or sinning will make us leave off praying. (1)

Lord, grant me one suit, which is this: Deny me all suits which are bad for me. (1)

Without prayer no work is well begun. (11)

He who copies the gods worships them adequately.

Our own method of worship, or habit of life, may be to us as a cherished staff on which we have long leaned, and which we have learned to love; let us not use it as a sword with which to vex and slay. (6)

Redemption is the science and the song of all eternity. (9)

Compassion will do more than passion.

God is where He was.

Who hath God, hath all; who hath Him not, hath less than nothing.

God waits to be gracious, and the gracious wait on God.

God loves us, not for what we are, but for what He can make us.

God's worst is better than the devil's best.

God hath promised to keep His people, and He will keep His promise.

When it pleaseth not God, the saint can do little. (99)

God, pervading all, is in all things the mystery of each. (62)

Mystery is God's great name; He is the mystery of each. (62)

Proverbs Worth Remembering.

A ragged colt may make a good horse.

The little alms are the good alms.

What none can prove a forgery may be true.

God can do without our learning, but He needs our ignorance still less. (123)

Our sorrows are never so great that they hide our mercies. (123)

God does not lose the details in the whole. (123)

Say "No," before you know it to your cost.

Our fidelity will not be without failures, nor our confidence without fears. (6)

Who would wish to be valued must make himself scarce.

All may do what has by man been done. (8)

The greatest things are done by the help of small ones.

The greatest oaks have been little acorns.

He that goes the contrary way must go over it twice.

It is not a chargeable thing to salute civilly.

The confidence of ability is ability. (123)

The truth which a man or a generation requires most is the truth which he or they like least. (123)

Envy and wrath shorten the life, and carefulness bringeth age before the time. (10)

Two things a man should never be an angry at; what he can help, and what he cannot help.

The solemn aspect of our passing days is that they are making us. (123)

He that will not be ruled by the rudder will be wrecked on the rock.

God's anger is His love thrown back upon itself from unreceptive and unloving hearts. (123)

The Lord is . . . slow to anger. (156)

He will not keep His anger for ever. (156)

A competence is all we can enjoy. (8)

That's not good language that all understand not.

Every time the sheep bleats it loses a mouthful.

True honor is acquired by nothing but good conduct. (21)

No man can safely govern that would not willingly become subject. (18)

Permanent and solid character is built up out of trivial actions. (123)

From a bad paymaster get what you can.

A little time may be enough to hatch great mischief.

By timely mending save much spending.

I not only speak so that I can be understood, but so that I cannot be misunderstood. (135)

Where there is much light the shade is deepest. (36)

That which was bitter to endure may be sweet to remember.

Any egg before an eagle, a thought before a thing. (62)

No one gets into trouble without his own help.

The rolling stone gathers no moss.

We do not always gain by changing.

Enthusiasm is essential to the triumph of truth.

It is tone that makes the music.

To follow foolish precedents, and wink with both our eyes, is easier than to think. (7)

It is an equal failing to trust everybody, and to trust nobody.

Bad excuses are worse than none.

Gain, when badly gotten, is sure to turn rotten.

God fills the empty, and empties the full.

He that wants looking after is not worth looking after.
It is too late to cover the well when the child is drowned.
It may be hard to work but it must be harder to want.
Before you spend elevenpence, earn a shilling.
Bad customs are not binding.
A fog cannot be dispelled by a fan.   (100)
We hate delay, yet it make us wise.
All is not lost that is delayed.
The hole invites the thief.
Keep the common road and you are safe.
He that makes himself an ass must not take it ill if men ride him.
Application makes the ass.
Do not call a fly an elephant.
The highest art is artlessness.   (91)

The Seven Sayings of Greece.

Look to the end of life.   (252)

Seize occasion.   (254)

The mean is best.   (253)

The most of men are evil.   (104)

Know thyself!   (200)

In industry is all.   (255)

Haste, if thou would'st fail.   (256)

The Seven Sayings of Golgotha.

Father, forgive them, for they know not what they do.
Today thou shalt be with me in paradise.
My God! My God! Why hast thou forsaken me?
Woman, behold thy son (looking at John)! Son, behold thy mother (looking at Mary)!
I thirst!
Into thy hands I commend my spirit.
It is finished.   (158)

A Parable.

An American traveler in Europe bought a first-class coach ticket for a day's ride through a mountainous country where there was no railroad.

After riding on the coach for sometime it occurred to him that he was very foolish to have bought a first-class ticket when all passengers fared alike. And so, with that famous American characteristic, he appealed to the driver as to "what he got on his first-class ride that the second and third class passengers did not?"

The driver assured him that his value would appear before the end of the journey and it was fully acknowledged when as they came to the bottom of a seven-mile hill, just after dinner, the driver threw down his reins and made this announcement: "First-class passengers, please keep your seats! Second-class passengers, get out and walk! Third-class passengers, get out and push!"

Merciless Truths.

The problem of attracting the whole world's attention without incurring the ridicule of anyone has never yet been solved.

When drink enters into a man's mouth and steals away his brains it would be mighty hard to convict the drink of anything more serious than petit larceny.

The fiction writer who makes all his characters come out right has made considerable improvement on the process of creation.

Some men have to be half drunk before they begin to act naturally. Then everybody says they are drunk.

The man who clings to steady work for wages all his life, when he might make something of himself independently, is a fool. So is the man who, believing the foregoing statement to be true, throws up a good job and fails to make a success of the independent venture. So take your choice.

Of all nature's quick processes, one of the most miraculous is that by which she instantaneously and indelibly labels the backboneless man as an easy mark.

The man with too little ability to accomplish a week's work in six days will make his failure still more completely by bungling away on Sunday.

Philosophers say that suppressed tendencies in parents crop out in children. On that hypothesis, men and women who suppress all their good tendencies ought to have angelically good offspring.

The proudest man in the world is the freshly bereaved widower. Man naturally rejoices in the notoriety he can secure by being, for even a few days, the center of a community's sympathy. And the worse he carries on the more praise he will get from his neighbors for having been a model husband.

Many a man who shows his wife the inside of his heart has blind doors in the inner walls. And no one except the man himself knows whither those blind passageways lead.

As is cauliflower to cabbage, so is repartee to "back talk."

High church and low church differ in several points, but in none more noticeably than that one has matins and the other carpets.

An ideal money-maker is a machine the details of which are diagrammed in the asbestos blue prints which paper the walls of hell. (258)

Casually considered, there is no appreciable difference between a swindler and a philanthropist; each is on the lookout for "good things to *do*."

The man who lives close to God never is heard bragging about his own holiness.

They who read but little are apt to have a penchant for reading what is not worth reading.

A clown in the pulpit, posing to make the people laugh, is an awful travesty on the high calling of preaching.

What would be the use of immortality to a person who cannot use well a half hour? (55)

A distinguished Chinese philosopher once said: "Those who know do not speak much; those who speak much do not know." Solomon put the same wise thought as follows: "Even a fool, when he holdeth his peace is counted wise." "And a fool's voice is known by multitude of words."

In these days of progress when that which we yesterday extolled to the skies is to-day quietly pushed aside, the only cry which pleases the heart of aspiring man is "FORWARD!" No matter to what branch of the arts and sciences one may devote his attention, something superior, something new, something hitherto unequaled must be evolved, or the outcome of thought and labor will be abortive.

It makes a deal of difference whether you retire from business or the business retires from you.

Keep pace with your day and generation.

The man who does not avail himself of modern methods is right at the outset giving himself a handicap that scarcely the wit of a Mark Twain or the genius of an Edison or ability of a Rockefeller can overcome.

Be up-to-date. The time has gone by when past success is considered an element of strength. In this day and age, experience counts for far less than it formerly did. This is an age of great progress—of rapid change. Experience is not needed so much as is courage to break away from old methods.

Though cobwebs of antiquity surround the saying "Wealth is the canker that destroys nations," must of us keep pretty well occupied in trying to corner the canker. Wealth may destroy nations, but we're all anxious to be "in at the death."

If a man can write a better book, preach a better sermon, or make a better mousetrap than his neighbor, though he build his house in the woods, the world will make a beaten path to his door. (55)

"Times are hard," you say. Well, what are you going to do about it? It is partly your own fault. Others are busy making money, why not you? Will you longer despair and make times harder for yourself, or will you show the grit of a live, wide-awake business man by hustling so much the harder for business and dollars? Times are largely what we make them, so far as our individuality is concerned. You can't make business any better by sitting down and mourning over "hard times." An hour's despondency saps one's energies more than a week's hustling after business. The man who drops by the wayside and gives up the battle without a struggle was never built for success. He doesn't deserve it.

Business Men's Philosophy.

Special privilege usually assassinates itself in the end.

Greed always paves the way for the downfall of those that make it the guiding star of their lives.

Greed leads to dalliance with dishonor. When other people's money is in trust greed has no scruples.

Lust for dishonest riches is its own Nemesis. It may fatten temporarily on an apathetic public conscience, but it commits hari-kari because it doesn't know when to stop.

That honesty pays, that public spirit pays, that trickery and dishonesty do not pay, are written in letters of fire.

There is no other standard of public prosperity or private weal than the simple one of character.

There are other things besides money, even in this dollar-chasing age. A clear conscience and the respect of one's fellow citizens are still worth striving for.

He who raises the black flag in any avenue of life is riding hard for a fall.

Retribution is not the highest of laws, human or divine, but it is as inexorable as fate.

On Man and Nation.

We must treat each man on his worth and merits as a man. We must see that each is given a square deal, because he is entitled to no more and should receive no less. (262)

Mankind goes ahead but slowly, and it goes ahead mainly through each of us trying to do the best that is in him, and to do it in the sanest way. (262)

We have in our scheme of government no room for the man who does not wish to pay his way through life by what he does for himself and for the community. (262)

When all is said and done, the rule of brotherhood remains as the indispensable prerequisite of success in the kind of national life for which we strive. (262)

The life of duty, not the life of mere ease or mere pleasure,— that is the kind of life which makes the great man, as it makes the great nation. (262)

The Government cannot supply the lack in any man of the qualities which must determine in the last resort the man's success or failure. (262)

A healthy republican government must rest upon individuals, not upon classes or sections. (262)

Far and away the best prize that life offers is the chance to work hard at work worth doing. (262)

I desire to see in this country the decent men strong and the strong men decent, and until we get that combination in pretty good shape we are not going to be by any means as successful as we should be. (262)

If we wish to make the State the representative and exponent and symbol of decency, it must be made through the decency, public and private, of the average citizen. (262)

To me the future seems full of hope because, although there are many conflicting tendencies, and although some of these tendencies of our present life are for evil yet, on the whole, the tendencies for good are in the ascendency. (262)

In our own country, with its many-sided hurrying, practical life, the place for cloistered virtue is far smaller than is the place for that essential manliness which without losing its fine and lofty side, can yet hold its own in the rough struggle with the forces of the world round about us. (262)

The line of cleavage between good citizenship and bad citizenship separates the rich man who does well from the rich man who does ill, the poor man of good conduct from the poor man of bad conduct. (262)

It is an infamous thing in our American life and fundamentally treacherous to our institutions, to apply to any man any test save that of his personal worth, or to draw between two sets of men any distinction save the distinction of conduct. (262)

In the first place, the man who makes a promise which he does not intend to keep, and does not try to keep, should rightly be adjudged to have forfeited in some degree what should be every man's most precious possession,—his honor. (262)

Succeed? Of course we shall succeed! How can success fail to come to a race of masterful energy and resoluteness which has a continent for the base of its domain, and which feels within its veins the thrill that comes to generous souls when their strength stirs in them, and they know that the future is theirs? (262)